Dear Teacher

Dear teacher, you are appreciated! This inspirational book, written by motivational speakers Brad Johnson and Hal Bowman, provides daily encouragement to thank you for all that you do in the classroom and beyond. Johnson and Bowman offer quotes and powerful stories for 100 days of the school year, highlighting topics such as celebrating small successes, bringing out the best in your students, knowing your worth, and being all in. The book is perfect for teachers of all grade levels, and for principals to buy their teachers for schoolwide morale, to keep teachers feeling their best. The uplifting advice will remind you why you've chosen this profession and the impact you have on others!

Brad Johnson has over 20 years of experience as a teacher and administrator at the K–12 and collegiate level. He is a national speaker and author and is also on the national faculty for Concordia University School of Graduate Studies in Leadership.

Hal Bowman is a renowned speaker, education consultant, and the creator of transformational programs like Teach Like a Rockstar and Be the One. Before becoming a full-time speaker, he spent over 20 years in K–12 classrooms, teaching everything from Band to Biology.

Dear Teacher

100 Days of Inspirational Quotes and Anecdotes

Brad Johnson and Hal Bowman

Routledge
Taylor & Francis Group

NEW YORK AND LONDON

First published 2021
by Routledge
52 Vanderbilt Avenue, New York, NY 10017

and by Routledge
2 Park Square, Milton Park, Abingdon, Oxon OX14 4RN

Routledge is an imprint of the Taylor & Francis Group, an informa business

Library of Congress Cataloging-in-Publication Data
Names: Johnson, Brad, 1969– author. | Bowman, Hal, author.
Title: Dear teacher: 100 days of inspirational quotes
and anecdotes / Brad Johnson, Hal Bowman.
Description: New York, NY: Routledge, 2021. |
Identifiers: LCCN 2020043269 (print) | LCCN 2020043270 (ebook) |
ISBN 9780367645809 (hardback) | ISBN 9780367622213 (paperback) |
ISBN 9781003125280 (ebook)
Subjects: LCSH: Teachers–Conduct of life. |
Motivation in education.
Classification: LCC LB1775 .J545 2021 (print) |
LCC LB1775 (ebook) | DDC 371.1–dc23
LC record available at https://lccn.loc.gov/2020043269
LC ebook record available at https://lccn.loc.gov/2020043270

ISBN: 978-0-367-64580-9 (hbk)
ISBN: 978-0-367-62221-3 (pbk)
ISBN: 978-1-003-12528-0 (ebk)

Typeset in Palatino LT Std
by Newgen Publishing UK

I dedicate this book to my first teacher, my mother (Carolyn Johnson). She taught me to read before I even started school and has never stopped teaching me lessons about life, compassion, and doing things the right way. Mom, thank you for all your support and encouragement through the years!

Love, Brad

Whenever I'm about to immerse myself in a new book, I always take a moment to read the dedication. It's usually a few sweet sentences about someone who has played an important and special role in the life of the author. I love mushy stuff like that, it warms my heart. Well, this dedication is extra-sweet and super-mushy because this book is dedicated to YOU – the person who serves in the most important and special role of all, teaching kids. So, as you hold this book in your hands and as it warms your heart, please accept it as a token of my deep appreciation for all you do for your students, our leaders of tomorrow who are sitting in your classroom today. Our world is a better place because of you.

Hal Bowman

Contents

Meet the Authors ix

Preface xi

100 Days of Quotes and Anecdotes 1

Brad's Days: 1–5, 11–15, 21–25, 31–35, 41–45, 51–59,
70–75, 81–85, 91–94, 100

Hal's Days: 6–10, 16–20, 26–30, 46–50, 60–69, 76–80,
86–90, 95–99

Meet the Authors

Dr. Brad Johnson is one of the most dynamic and engaging speakers in the fields of education and leadership. He has 25 years of experience in the trenches as a teacher and administrator. Dr. Johnson is transforming how teachers lead in the classroom and how administrators lead in the school. He is a servant- leader who shares his vast experiences and expertise to help other educators maximize their potential. He is the author of many books, including *Principal Bootcamp, Putting Teachers First,* and *Learning on Your Feet.* He has traveled the globe speaking and training teachers and educational leaders.

After 20 years in the classroom, **Hal Bowman** has spent the last decade inspiring hundreds of thousands of educators, delivering effective tools and strategies that transform classroom and campus culture. He is the creator of four unique programs: *Teach Like a Rock Star, Hal Bowman's Be the One, Change a Kid's Life,* and *Shout It from the Rooftops.* Onstage, Hal's highpowered, lively keynotes and events have revolutionized professional development in education, offering a refreshing approach that inspires teachers to reconnect with their passion for changing their students' lives in profound and meaningful ways. Online, Hal reaches countless educators each week as the host of the *Teach Like a Rock Star Podcast* and *Help a Teacher Facebook Live with Hal Bowman.* He is also the founder of *Men in Education,* an online platform for educators providing community, personal growth, and professional development, addressing the unique roles men can play in the lives of students. Hal has committed his life to keeping his finger on the ever-changing pulse of education in America. He lives happily in Houston, Texas with his wife and two kids. He also shares his home with a few furry four-legged creatures who are not moved, in the least, by his inspirational prowess.

Preface

Dear Teacher,

Over the years, I have seen many changes in education, such as technology, curriculum, and other innovations, but the one constant that has always been the backbone of education is the hardworking and dedicated teacher. In fact, very few people will ever understand the time, energy, commitment, and sacrifice that you make for your students. It's why most teachers say it's a calling.

You are never fully appreciated for the countless hours you spend in the evenings and on the weekends to prepare lessons and grade work; or for spending your own money on school supplies. You spend your summers reading, taking PD's, implementing new curricula, and fixing up your classroom, all without pay! I know of no other profession which expects that of their professionals. And even above and beyond that, you often become emotionally invested in the well-being of your students. You care about them, you worry about them, and you even lose sleep over them.

In my 25 years, I have worked with some of the most amazing teachers and administrators. Teachers who could easily lead a school or school district but choose to stay in the classroom because they love impacting their students daily. You are not just educating students, but you are helping build our future. There is no nobler profession.

So, hopefully this book will encourage, inspire, and even validate you as a teacher. And let you know how much we appreciate you. Even your students, whether or not they ever tell you, are thankful and appreciative for all you do for them. Many students wish they could say thank you, or let you know that you are their hero because of the influence you have had on their lives.

May each quote and anecdote speak to you, encourage you, and let you know that you are right where you need to be, which is in the classroom teaching students, loving students, and influencing the next generation to be better because you were their teacher! You may not always see the fruit of your labor, but as the cover of this book suggests, you are planting seeds of knowledge, hope, and love that will live on forever!

Brad Johnson

1

"Love What You Teach, but Love Who You Teach More"

I love to share my observation that elementary teachers love their students, high school teachers love their subject, and college instructors love themselves. Oh, and middle school teachers love chaos and wine! This gets a nice chuckle when I speak, mainly because middle school teachers can relate to the chaos of middle school students. However, the reality is to be an effective teacher, you should enjoy what you teach, but always love who you teach the most.

Now, this doesn't mean that you will like every student. In fact, you will have some students who will get on your last nerve and drive you crazy, but that doesn't mean you don't love them as a human or want the best for them. In fact, those are the ones who need love the most. In my 25 years in education, I found that students who I didn't connect with usually were the ones who acted out or tried to get attention in unhealthy ways, like disrupting class. Therefore, I learned early on that I needed to focus on connections before I focused on content. Throughout the years, this helped alleviate many behavioral issues in class. When you develop that rapport with students, there really isn't a better job in the world. When I think about my years teaching, I did enjoy teaching science, but I loved the kids, and the kids are the one thing I miss most about teaching in the K-12 setting.

So, you do need a genuine affection for kids in general or you will never survive a career as a teacher. When you think of the long hours, the planning, the weekends spent making lessons, the money you spend out of your own pocket on resources, you realize you do it because you love your students. That is why most teachers don't refer to them as their class or their students, but call them, "My Kids." Because for the year you are fortunate to be with them, they are indeed, your kids, and you love them!

2

"Relationships Before Rigor, Grace Before Grades, Patience Before Programs, Love Before Lessons"

Remember how education was thrown upside down when the pandemic first hit in March 2020? Teachers were expected to jump from a traditional school setting to the virtual world. I received messages from teachers all around the globe who were frustrated, stressed out, and in tears. Many were questioning their own ability and if they should even stay in teaching. You may have been one of those teachers. So I came up with the quote above to end a tweet that I sent out. It was well received by administrators and teachers across the country.

The purpose was to help focus on what was important during a time of crisis and that even in education there were priorities more important than our traditional focus. For instance, how important is rigor when many students may not be able to access the internet, or are busy taking care of siblings at home. While it is easier to see things differently during a crisis, my question was: Why isn't this the priority all the time?

So while you do have high expectations for your students and want them to give their best, remember that they are human first, and when you focus on things like building relationships and patience, they will actually work harder and be more successful. Students work harder for teachers they like and who like them. Let this quote be your motto for the rest of the year and the rest of your career!

3

Teachers, Be Memorable to Your Students; Just Make Sure It Is a Good Memory

Most teachers I have surveyed over the years attribute their desire to become a teacher to one of their teachers. Most remember fondly a teacher who brought out a passion for a subject, or who believed in them when others did not. I can still recall just about every teacher I had, but I have never forgotten the few who made a positive impact on my life. Ms. Mueller was my 7th grade science teacher and the teacher who had the greatest influence on me in school. She not only made science fun, but she had fun review games where she gave away prizes, such as UGA Bulldog cups full of candy. I was a good student, but I studied extra hard to win those prizes during review games. Ironically, I taught middle grades science for many years and I also made sure to have fun review games, along with the occasional prizes!

I also remember an experience during my second-year teaching where a colleague let me know one of her students, who I taught and coached, had written a paper about me in her English class. The paper was about someone they most admired. I won't bore you with the contents of the paper, but let's just say this big lug was in tears. He never told me about it and I never let him know that I was given a copy by his teacher, but it was an honor to know that I had impacted a student's life and that in so doing he had impacted my life as well. It is something that

I never forgot. But it was something I would have never known, if she hadn't been willing to share with me. Remember that you are an important influence on your students' lives and they will never forget you, just make sure the memories that they have of you are good ones!

4

You Are the Difference Maker!

Did you know that you are the most important factor in the success of your students in the classroom this year? I interviewed the Georgia State Superintendent, Kathy Cox, a few years ago about the importance of relationships in the classroom. You may remember her name because she became the first million-dollar winner on the American television game show *Are You Smarter Than a 5th Grader*? She had conducted extensive research on the topic and shared with me in an interview that, "Nothing is more important to the student's success than a positive relationship with the teacher regardless of interferences to their education such as a tough home life, limited parental support or socio-economic level" (*The Edutainer, Johnson*, 2010).

I have often said that it is not the technology or the curriculum, but it is the teacher that makes education successful. So, while you may not have control over technology, curriculum, or other resources, realize you are the Most Valuable Resource for your students. You are the difference maker! Create a learning environment that is fun, challenging, and supportive. Students will work harder for someone they like and respect. Think of how a child wants to please their parents. Students will do the same for a teacher with whom they have built a positive relationship. Make relationships your priority from day one, let them know you believe in them and it will make the rest of the year more effective!

5

You Are Not in Competition

My motto for schools is that the best team wins. Unfortunately, in some schools there seems to be a culture of competition. Whether it's between teachers trying to decorate their room the best or create the best lessons. While there is nothing inherently wrong with this, I believe this is sometimes done in an attempt to get attention from administrators who may not show enough support and appreciation for their staff.

But remember, you are part of a team and not in competition with each other. You don't need to be just like or better than the teacher down the hall. But it is ok to learn from other teachers, especially if they do something really well. I learned as much my first year teaching from teammates, than I did during my whole teacher preparation program. So don't be afraid to share ideas with your colleagues and don't be afraid to ask for ideas from your colleagues.

Most importantly when you realize that you are a team, you will be more willing to encourage, support, and inspire your colleagues. Motivate each other, build each other up, and help each other succeed. This doesn't just mean your fellow teachers, but even staff and administrators would love some support and encouragement from you as well.

6

Surround Yourself with Those Teachers You Need, as Well as Those Teachers Who Need You

In just about every profession, outside of teaching, you would receive the same advice: "If you want to be successful, surround yourself with the best and stay clear of the rest."

That advice is based on the theory that we become the average of the people we spend most of our time with. To an extent, I think that's probably true – especially in a professional setting. Let's face it, if you sell insurance you should probably spend time with the best salespeople so that you can learn, grow, and become successful. Just as important, stay clear of "the rest", as you're certainly not going to learn effective strategies and best practices by surrounding yourself with those who are struggling.

It all makes perfect sense. But, teaching is dramatically different. It's different because in our profession those educators who are struggling are in classrooms teaching and influencing our children every day.

So, it's not just about the ineffectiveness of those teachers. It's more about the students who suffer as a result. In education, our motto is different: "Surround yourself with the best, so you can influence the rest. First, surround yourself with the most positive, passionate, and effective educators. Then, one by one, pull "the rest" into your circle so they can learn from "the best".

That approach is what's best for you. It's what's best for teachers who are struggling. And, most importantly, it's best for our kids.

7

It Just about Takes a Felony for Me to Send a Kid to the Office; This is Our Family, We Handle It in Here

I have two children, both teenagers. Just like all kids, they've had a few behavior issues throughout their childhoods. Nothing "bad." Just typical, teenage-kid-trying-to-figure-it-all-out kind of stuff.

Suppose during one of those parenting moments when things getting increasingly tense, and emotions were running high, and voices were escalating, my approach were to scream at my son, "If you don't stop right now, I will call Ms. Sabuco the president of the homeowners association and let her handle this!"

How absurd would that be? We love Ms. Sabuco and she does a great job at running the homeowner's association. However, she's not his parent; she's not a part of our immediately family; and, she doesn't understand the dynamics of our family.

It's the same thing when it comes to sending a kid to the office or calling the principal down to the classroom to handle behavior issues.

When we push our behaviorally challenging students onto an administrator to handle, we are sending a clear message to every student in the class that this is not our family and this teacher is not really our leader.

Our students need to feel that they are a part of a family that's lead by a teacher who will love and take care of them, both in their best times and their worst.

8

You Can't Pick and Choose Which Kid Needs You and Which Kid Doesn't, Your Students Will Forever Be Better Actors than You Are a Teacher

As soon as I walked into the school cafetorium to attend my students' 10 Year Reunion, we picked up right where we left off a decade earlier when I was a first-year teacher. The feeling of being together, the personalities, the inside jokes – it was as if nothing had changed.

But, as we sat around talking late into the night, everything changed.

The kids who grew up in rural, extreme poverty remembered their childhoods with such happiness and joy as they talked about the closeness, love, and support of their families.

Many of the kids who grew up at a higher socio-economic level talked about their incredibly painful childhoods that were filled with abuse, alcoholism, and fear.

After 10 years of teaching I finally made the realization. Students may grow up with two parents who have awesome jobs and take them to club soccer and youth group in a fancy car and live in a big, beautiful house with a labradoodle in the front yard. But, you'll never really know what's truly happening inside of that home.

Never will you know for sure which kids need you and which kids don't. It's all of them. Every single one. Every single day.

9

You're Not Just Teaching Kids What You Know; They're Becoming Who You Are

It seems we've all had that student in class who, when we think back, our memories are highlighted with his frustration, sadness, anger, mistakes, outbursts, and an epic melt down or two. You wonder to yourself, "I had that kid in my class for an entire school year. Did he even learn anything at all?"

He absolutely did.

Decades from now, when that boy has grown into a productive young man, raising his own children, he's going to be faced with difficult parenting moments.

When his children are frustrated, he's going to encourage them. When his children are sad, he's going to console them. When his children are angry, he'll be understanding. When his children make mistakes, he'll give them another chance. When his children have outbursts, he'll be patient. When his children are in the midst of an epic meltdown and crying uncontrollably, he's going to hold them close and tell them he loves them.

And, he's going to do it all because he learned it from you.

10

Please Don't Compare Your Chapter 1 to Another Teacher's Chapter 30

Teaching might be the only profession on the planet where a first year, first day educator is expected to live up to the same expectations of a 30-year veteran of the classroom. That is, on day one of her career, a brand new teacher is expected to teach the same content with the same level of effectiveness and her kids will be assessed with the same standardized tests while being expected to have the same achievement scores as the teacher down the hall with decades of experience.

Well, I can tell you that after traveling around the country and getting to know some of our nation's greatest educators, I've come to the conclusion that they all have a couple things in common. First, time in the classroom. And, second, many, many years of collaborating with other teachers. Neither of which is possible for a first day teacher.

Just like any great novel, chapter 1 of a teacher's career should be all about learning how to set the stage for a story that will be filled with incredibly colorful characters, unimaginable events, seemingly insurmountable challenges, and page-turning plot twists you never saw coming.

And, if you're the 30-year veteran, take the time to play the role of the influential protagonist who takes a struggling, young educator under your wing and mentors them as they begin composing the first chapter of their career.

11

You Don't Have to Be Perfect to Be Great!

Often, because teachers are almost perfectionists, you may begin to think that "great" isn't as good as "perfect," and that perfection is actually attainable. In contrast, mere high achievers tend to do better than their perfectionistic counterparts because they are generally less stressed and are satisfied with a job well done. They don't pick it apart and try to zero in on what could have been better.

This means give your best and it will be more than enough. It also means you don't have to be perfect to make a difference in the lives of your students or your colleagues. I believe that teachers have a built-in guilt gene, that makes us our worst critics. But, we need to learn to let go of perfection! You don't need to have your life all together to help others. In fact some of the times that you will be most encouraging or inspiring to others is when you are dealing with your own issues. It is our humanity that makes us relatable to others. We can identify with others through their hardships and through our own. However, the beauty of focusing on others, even when you don't have it all together is that it will often make you feel better yourself!

There is an old saying that perfection is the enemy of greatness. I believe that when we focus too much on being perfect, we actually burnout because of unrealistic expectations and wind-up performing less than effective. Be comfortable with your best, not with perfection!

12

Stay Young at Heart

Teaching is often called one of the hardest jobs in America. While working with students can be rewarding, it can also be hard work. So, one of the most important qualities of a teacher is to stay young at heart. Once you stop enjoying time with the kids, laughing often, and enjoying the little things, then you will lose the joy of teaching.

I love when I hear teachers who have been in the classroom for 15, 20, or even 25 years say that they couldn't imagine doing anything else. These are the teachers who are still young at heart. I have been fortunate to travel all around the country and I can say with confidence that the best teacher I ever taught with was a friend of mine named Tammy McElroy. Even after two decades of teaching, she was still as excited at the beginning of each school year as the year before. Her students loved coming to her class. She had high expectations of her students, but she also knew how to reach them on their level so they would be successful. She also loved to have fun. She was always creating fun games, and when an adult came into her room, they would have to answer a question before entering. The students loved this because she would ask hard questions that teachers and administrators would usually miss but the students would know. So they would shout the answer and feel so good about themselves! Needless to say I didn't enter her class very often! To stay young at heart, try to do something that scares you every day, forget about acting your age and just act like yourself, and finally, never stop adding curiosity and wonderment to learning.

13

What is Your Inner Recorder Playing?

Teaching is still a very isolating profession. You spend more time alone with students than with colleagues. This means you spend most of your day talking to yourself. In fact, most of our conversations throughout a day are with ourself. So what is it that you're telling yourself?

Our self-talk or inner recording can affect our effectiveness as a teacher/leader. Too often our self-talk may be negative. What happens after you've done something embarrassing? Does your inner voice say, "Well that was dumb?" What if you haven't even done anything wrong, but your self-talk is just as critical? "Don't speak up now and show everyone you don't know."

This **destructive** type of self-talk causes you to question yourself, so that you can soon become paralyzed with doubt and uncertainty. Ultimately, you are your only competition. It is not a competitor or someone else it is only you competing with yourself to be the best you can be.

Self-talk should be beneficial. It should be encouraging you to do your best, to be your best. For some people, self-talk is about identifying your purpose. What is it that you offer that no one else does? What talents or abilities do you bring to the table?

When you realize you do have assets to bring to your leadership role, then you need to encourage yourself often! Self-talk or the recorder shouldn't just be playing occasionally. It should be in constant loop mode, where you are continually telling yourself that you are the woman, you are the man, you can do it! Your recorder can influence as much as 99% of your success!

14

Celebrate Small Successes

When you are working with students, especially younger students, never take anything for granted. It's important to celebrate small successes. Think of the student who finally understood a math concept, or got their first A on an exam. In the big picture of life, these successes may not seem like much, but in that moment they are huge!

Often we wait until the end of the semester, or year, or some other "big event" to celebrate successes, such as academic awards. Well, over time, the small wins will be forgotten and seem unimportant. Recognizing these small wins is as much about being timely as anything else. In the moment, they help keep us inspired and moving forward. It can be hard to build momentum, so start with small wins.

The best way to have a successful year is to secure small wins, because small wins often make a huge difference. These small wins make work more meaningful and inspire us to continue forward. So, if you have a student who finally starts interacting in class, or improves their grade, then celebrate! A student who finally understands a concept in math or science deserves an 'atta boy! Affirmation is critical to overall success and even the small wins are wins! Celebrate the small successes because they transform moments into the momentum for great things. Even as adults, we like to be recognized for a job well done and students are certainly no different.

15

Failure Is a Comma, Not a Period.

I am not sure where this thought originated, but it has been a motto I have used throughout life. I remember sharing this once and a teacher said, "I love punctuation inspiration!" Apparently, she was an English teacher, so I am glad I got the punctuation right.

You may be struggling right now in your own life. You may feel like you are failing your students, or failing your family, or failing to keep a healthy balance between work and school. Just know that while you may feel like you're failing, it doesn't make you a failure and it doesn't mean that it is permanent. It seems to be human nature that we focus on what we don't do well rather than what we do well. And this doesn't mean we should take failure lightly, I think it's important to always try our best and to succeed, but there are times when we learn as much from failure as we do success.

In the sports world, especially for youth sports, there's a saying that there is no winning or losing, just winning and learning. I think this is important for us to remember as adults and to teach our students as well. The focus shouldn't be just about the outcome but growing and learning from the process. When you feel like you have failed, stop and take a breath! Reflect, make adjustments, and then continue to move forward. Failure isn't fatal or final, it is just a pause or a learnable moment on the road to success.

16

Just a Few Words Spoken at the Right Moment Can Change a Kid's Life Forever

As educators we've all sat through back to school professional development sessions where an administrator outlined some big, complex, strategic approach to making a difference in the lives of students. Typically, it involved charts and graphs, research-based best practices, and acronyms. Lots and lots of acronyms.

I remember one year we were even given the acronym – TEMPERATURE – to help us remember the 11 positive behavior expectations. I love that we invested so much in helping our kids to develop into amazing people. I think our hearts were definitely in the right place. But today, after talking with hundreds of former students, who are now almost 40 years old, never has a single one of them said to me, "I remember that year all the teachers constructed six foot, full color, elaborate thermometers to rate and score our behavior TEMPERATURE on campus. That truly made a difference in my life!" Not a single one.

Instead, they talk about the simplest moments I never imagined would have mattered so much. "I'll never forget that day in the hallway when you held onto my shoulders, looked me right in the eye, and told me, 'I believe in you. I'm proud of you. And, I love you.'"

We can create the most sophisticated, beautiful themes for our classrooms that would look spectacular on Pinterest. However, truly making a difference in the life of a child will always come down to one thing: Taking the time to create those simple one-on-one, positive, emotional moments for students that build a relationship that lasts a lifetime.

17

Every Next Level of Teaching Will Require a Next Level of You

Thousands of pages from dozens of studies by countless researchers have all come to the same conclusion: The single most-important determining factor in the academic success of your students is you, their teacher – the one person who has accepted the honor and privilege of standing before kids, day after day, and leading them on their educational journeys.

The evidence of that research leads to the logical conclusion that, "If I'm to become a master educator, I need to master instructional pedagogy."

While the correlation between "an increase in knowledge equals an increase in results" may be true in other professions, I haven't found it to be true in the classroom. I think we've all seen teachers who are constantly attending professional development sessions who never really get better at their craft.

Teaching isn't only about the process of transferring knowledge more effectively from your brain to the student's brain. It's more about empowering kids to grow into kind, capable adults of exceptional character who just so happen to be extremely knowledgeable.

I've seen amazing math teachers who aren't mathematicians. But, I've never seen an educator mold a child into a young adult of exceptional character who wasn't a teacher of exceptional character.

We must be constantly learning and growing to become who we want our students to become.

18

Your Students Desperately Need to Know Why You Teach

Imagine a student asks you, "Why do you teach?"

If you're like most teachers, you probably have a couple of answers to that question. One answer is at the top of your mind – a quick-and-easy, effortless answer. The other answer is in your heart. That one is neither quick nor easy, and it may take some effort to uncover it, or maybe even discover it for the first time.

Let's do an exercise together to bring the answer from your heart up into your mind.

First, as quick as you can, write down your top of the mind, quick-and-easy answer to the question, "Why do you teach?"

Now, as you consider what you wrote, ask yourself the question, "Why is that?" You'll find the answer to that second question is a little bit deeper than your first answer.

Then, with that second, slightly deeper answer clear in your mind, again, ask yourself the question, "Why is that?" And, again, you'll find an even deeper answer.

Continue that process as many times as you need to get to the deepest, most real, answer of all – the one in your heart. You'll know when you're there because when you ask yourself the question, "Why is that?" for the final time, there is no answer. That's just what it is.

If you're like most great teachers, the final answer will be some form of, "Because I love my kids."

19

Let's Not Make It More Complicated than It Needs to Be; Send Your Kids Home Each Afternoon Just a Tiny Bit Better than They Came to You That Morning

Even after just a few years of teaching, we tend to get a little jaded when it comes to welcoming in the newest, latest-and-greatest, school-wide initiative for increasing academic achievement. With each new program we adopt it seems they get increasingly complex and scientific sounding. Maybe the thought is that the more complicated and technical it sounds, the more teachers will believe it might actually work.

I think about student change in a much more simplified way.

Imagine a pilot takes off from the runway, but their flightpath is off by just a microscopic fraction of an inch. Thousands of miles and hours later she is going to end up in a completely different place than where she originally expected. That's how I approach redirecting the trajectory of a kid's path in life. I'm just trying to send my kids home each day just a tiny bit better than they came to me that morning. Because if I can shift a kid's path in life just a little bit in a positive direction, even just a microscopic nudge, I might not see the results today but over the next few decades of life that kid is going to end up in a whole different world than anyone ever expected.

20

We Underestimate What It Takes for Children to Pull Themselves Up Out of a Chaotic Home Life That's Immersed in Poverty; It Will Simply Never Happen without Help

Robin Miller is one of my favorite teachers in the nation. Her understanding of kids who come from poverty is astounding. She says, "If you stop thinking about it as 'generational poverty' and start thinking about it as 'genetic poverty' you will understand how those kids feel. Overcoming 'generational poverty' feels difficult. Overcoming 'genetic poverty' feels impossible."

Obviously, Robin does not believe that being "poor" is genetic. Her point is that asking a kid to believe his life could be anything other than one that's immersed in poverty is asking him to forget everything he knows to be true and to accept a completely different reality of the world.

I'm short. At 5'3", I'm about the height of a typical 7th grader. With that in mind, telling a kid from poverty, "All you need to do is make good grades so you can have a good job, a beautiful home, and a happy family" is no different than someone telling me, "All you need to do is grow taller."

Both statements feel equally impossible.

The difference is: Changing the reality of kids is possible. It's the result of daily, consistent effort by the person who loves them unconditionally, believes in them relentlessly, and is there for them at every turn.

That person is you.

21

Be World Class You!

I don't think I have ever given a speech where I didn't include this concept. I am by nature a maximizer influencer, which means that my strengths are to help people recognize their own strengths and maximize them! If you focus on developing your talents and passions then you can become your world class self! So often teachers feel like they have to copy a teacher down the hall or an expert they heard speak, but you don't need to be a copy of anyone, you simply need to be your best self.

They say there are two important days in your life: the day you were born and the day you realize why you born. We were all born with purpose. Our purpose is typically found when we identify and develop our talents and our passions. We have discussed the importance of helping teachers find their strengths so that they will be more successful in their personal and professional life. But there is not much more inspiring than living out your purpose. When teachers identify their strengths and passions and utilize them in the classroom and school community, then they will be inspired and be inspiring to everyone else.

The Formula Is Simply: Strengths + Passions = Purpose

What are your strengths, or things you do well? What are your passions, or things that stir your emotions? When you can combine strengths and passions you can live out your purpose. Many teachers feel that teaching is a calling, which means it is your purpose. So, focus on developing your best self, become a world class you! You will be more inspired and invigorated in your teaching and you will help your students reach their potential as well!

22

Gratitude Determines Your Attitude

The most successful people that I have interviewed over the years start their day with quiet time or reflection of gratitude. This can be done upon rising early each morning, before the rush of the day begins as we and maybe the family get ready and then sit in rush hour traffic to get to school. I always preferred, as a teacher, to get to school a few minutes early and use the time then to focus and prepare for the day. I would leave 20 minutes early and use that time in my classroom before students arrived as my quiet time. This worked well because I was on time and didn't need to worry about running in late, and secondly, I needed to de-stress from the drive into work.

What is the purpose of quiet time? To focus and prepare for the day. A great way to use quiet time is to focus on gratitude. What are you grateful for in your life? Your family, job, friends, and even your health? Starting the day with gratitude is like filling up your tank for the day! It will be the fuel to get you through the roughest of days.

Next focus on something you accomplished yesterday. Remember that momentum is important in life, so reflecting on a success from the day before will put you in the mindset of success and help focus on being successful today as well. Small successes, especially in education are a great motivator, even for a veteran teacher.

Finally, focus on your goals for the day. It is hard to know if you had a successful day if you don't have measurable goals. These don't have to be big goals, but I have found when I was able to achieve even small goals in a day, I felt much more successful and, yes, even grateful.

23

Don't Just Make an Impression; Make an Impact

We make impressions upon people every day. How we look, how we talk, even how we dress can all make an impression upon someone. But how often do you make an impact? What is the difference between impression and impact?

An **impression** is a vague notion, remembrance, or perception of someone. An **impact,** on the other hand, is to actually create a change in yourself or someone else.

Impressions are more temporary and superficial than an impact. But it is the one we are trained to focus on. Think about the old adage, you only get one chance to make a first impression. We feel this pressure when we interview for a job, go on a date, or stand in front of our class on the first day. But impressions can change and even be forgotten (thank goodness!) over time because they are more temporary. As it relates to you as a teacher, we will say that leaving an **impact is to have a strong and positive effect on someone**.

Most of you got into teaching because of a teacher who impacted your life. Many teachers may have left an impression on you, such as being funny, a good listener, genuinely caring, but the ones you remember best made some kind of impact. They were the ones who taught you to believe in yourself, celebrated your successes, genuinely cared for you, and even told you that you had talents and abilities to be successful. Be that teacher for your students. Never get so focused on the process of teaching that you forget the ones you are teaching. Yes, it's important to make a first impression, but it's so much more important to make a lasting impact!

24

Stop Underestimating Yourself

How many times have you doubted yourself or your abilities? Actually, let me rephrase, how many times this week have you doubted yourself or your abilities? It seems to be human nature that we underestimate our own abilities. We are in fact our own worst critic. And after 25 years in education, I believe teachers are some of the worst at underestimating themselves.

However, there may actually be a reason for that. Did you know teachers, more than any other profession, feel like their voice is least heard, and that their input is least listened to by administration? This means the average teacher doesn't feel supported or appreciated, which can lead to feelings of inadequacies and underestimating your abilities and what you bring to the classroom. So, when you are confronted with a new or stressful task or situation, you may begin to doubt your talents, strengths, or abilities. **Underestimating yourself** can cause anxiety or stress, and it may **prevent** you from being your most effective in the classroom and beyond.

How can you start seeing your true self, which is strong and capable? Remind yourself of all the amazing talents and abilities you bring to the classroom. Keep reminders of your achievements and successes, surround yourself with positive people, and finally focus on self-care. Often we feel worse about ourselves when we are run down, stressed, or overwhelmed. When you feel good physically, it often helps you feel better mentally and emotionally. Remember the old adage; you can't pour from an empty cup, well an empty cup causes us to underestimate ourselves as well.

25

Decision Fatigue

In education, we often joke there is tired, and then there is teacher tired. I don't think many people understand this truth, unless you have survived the first week or weeks of school. For the first few years of teaching, I remember going home after school and falling asleep for hours. Sometimes bed time was before sunset.

One of the reasons that teachers feel so worn out is because of **decision fatigue**. Research has found that teachers make more minute-by-minute decisions than brain surgeons, and that's extremely tiring. And the brain surgeon doesn't have to deal with a classroom full of students. In fact, a quiet operating room, where everything is clean and the patient is asleep, would be a dream workplace for most teachers!

Wait, back to reality! So, every choice you must make throughout the day taxes your mind and reduces your ability to make good decisions later in the day. Not to mention that you are trying to engage, entertain, and educate a classroom of children. That's why there are days when you go home and you are so exhausted that you don't feel like doing anything around the house, except taking a nap on the sofa. So how can you help alleviate some of this teacher tired? Create routines and organize so you have less decisions to make through the day. Make sure you are getting adequate sleep. Make healthier food choices and while time is a precious commodity, try to include exercise as much as possible. Finally, on days you feel the need, fall asleep on the sofa when you get home. Trust, me none of us will judge you!

26

Please Don't Just Walk By a Young, Struggling Teacher; Stop, Help, Encourage, and Mentor

As I think back over the course of my career, we did an amazing job welcoming our young, new teachers to our campus and the profession. The days leading up to the first day of school were filled with encouragement, support, and hospitality. Honestly, most schools I visit seem to do a good job of that.

But then the students arrive, reality sets in, and we immediately fall into the daily, chaotic routine of the school year. That's when it all starts to fall apart for our new teachers as they are left alone in their classrooms, silently struggling.

The reason our new teachers struggle so desperately is because we place the exact same expectations on a first-day teacher with no experience as we do a seasoned, veteran, expert educator with years of experience. Can you imagine how monumentally challenging that must feel in this day and age of teaching? From content delivery, to classroom management, to logistical processes and procedures, the first-day teacher has no real-world experience with any of it. As a result, they consistently question themselves and feel inadequate as they are unsure about every single thing they do. In fact, because they're so lost and uncertain, they don't even know what to ask or how to ask for help. That's why when you ask new teachers how they're doing, you can see the panic in their eyes as they answer, "It's fine. I'm fine. Everything is fine."

Nothing is "fine." I promise.

The new teachers on your campus need more than a mentor. They need a team of compassionate, intentional, and supportive educators to check on them every day. They desperately need people to help, encourage, and mentor them every day. But, please don't ask them, "What can I help you with today?" They're so deep in the struggle of learning how to be a teacher, they have no idea of what they need help with. So, just start helping. Just like when you first started teaching, they need help with everything.

27

The Double-Whammy of a Lie We Tell Our Students: "I'll Be Your Teacher This Year"

Isn't it amazing how we can squeeze two giant lies inside of one, tiny, six-word sentence? Sometimes we even tell those same two lies in one word, like when a kid asks, "Are you my teacher this year?" Without hesitation we immediately answer, "Yes." Two lies in a single word.

The first lie: "I'll be your teacher …"

"Teacher" may be the job title, but it's certainly not the job description. More accurately the job description should be, "Become the most influential person in the lives of your students as you serve to meet whatever individual needs those children may have." We can still use "Teacher" as the job title just so long as we all understand that title also includes parent, friend, counselor, advocate, confidant, guide, cheerleader, mentor, provider, and role model. And, that's just a fraction of the full list.

The second lie: "… this year."

Serving as a student's teacher is not something that only happens 180 days per year, during school hours, Monday through Friday. It's a permanent commitment between two human beings that lasts a lifetime. So, the next time a kid asks, "Are you my teacher this year?" Take a moment, get your thoughts together, and answer honestly. "I'm going to be one of the most influential people you'll ever have in your life and the work we do together will impact how you think, what you do, and who you are forever."

28

It Only Takes a Second to Say the Words, but the Impact Lasts Forever

Walking through Chicago's Midway Airport I heard him scream my name, "BOWMAN!" It had been 19 years since the last time I heard it, but I knew exactly who it was. Without even seeing him, I immediately yelled back, "TREVON!"

Nineteen years earlier, every single day for an entire school year I heard Trevon scream my name at the top of his lungs on his way to my second-period class. Sometimes he did it as he was entering my room. Sometimes he did it from the far end of the hall. Other times he even screamed from a few hallways over. And, every day, without fail, I would yell his name back as loud as I could.

As he ran toward me in the airport, I could see that he kept that same smile and enthusiasm for life as he transitioned from a boy to man. After reminiscing for a few minutes, he said,

> You know what I think about sometimes? The day when you and I were sitting on the curb after school and you looked over at me and said, 'I'm proud of you.' That meant the world to me. I'll never forget that.

It's incredible to think of all the lessons, the content, the projects, and the field trips we had together and what he remembers most of all is the three seconds it took for me to look him in the eye and say four words.

Sometimes we fall into believing that making a lifelong impact can only be the result of complex, strategic, research-based plans. When, in fact, it can happen with just a few words, in a few seconds.

Looking back, I regret that I didn't take more opportunities to look kids in the eye and tell them what they needed to hear.

Teach in such a way that you'll never have those regrets. It only takes a few seconds to say a few words to create a memory that will last a lifetime.

29

You Must Be Willing to Trade Immediate Gratification for Lifelong Impact

I watched a TV show about how a celebrity chef and his team would "take over" and transform a small town restaurant. From the menu to the décor, they would completely create a new restaurant overnight as hidden cameras were installed to capture the reactions of their unknowing, regular customers the next day.

When the patrons showed up for dinner the following day, they were immediately taken aback by the obvious and dramatic changes. People tasted their food and were amazed – beside themselves with excitement! Diners passed plates from table to table as they yelled to each other, "Roger, take a bite of this pork chop!" And, "Marcia, come over here and taste my salmon. It'll change your life!"

At the end of the show, the celebrity chef stepped out from the kitchen, everyone immediately recognized him, and people completely lost their minds. There was a standing ovation as people cheered and cried out, "Thank you so much!" "You're incredible!" and, "This is the best day of my life!"

As teachers, rarely, if ever, do we receive that kind of instant, positive feedback. I can't remember a single time when students cheered and cried out to me, "Thank you so much!" "You're incredible!" and, "This was the best day of my life!" at the end of a lesson.

But I do know this. The customers in the restaurant all went home that night, back to their normal, everyday lives. Was it a great experience? Sure. But, nothing really changed. In the end, they were all the same people living their same lives.

The difference for us, as teachers, is that all that we serve our students lasts a lifetime. Would we love some instant gratification at the end of every lesson? Sure. But, the real question is, are you willing to trade instant gratification for lifelong impact?

If you're anything like me, you'll make that trade every time.

Most importantly, I seriously doubt a piece of salmon has the power to change a life. But I know for sure that you do.

30

It's the Kid Who Behaves the Least Who Needs You the Most

It had been an incredibly hard day in the classroom which ended in a one-on-one yelling match with my student, Javier. Yelling was often my go-to instructional strategy as an immature, inexperienced, and ill-prepared first-year teacher. The last bell of the day rang at 3:00pm and I had had enough. I was in my car to leave by 3:03pm. As I started my car, I heard my principal, Dr. Jack Rhodes, yell from across the parking lot, "Wow, you're out of here early today!" I rolled down my window and described my day, along with the verbal sparring with Javier.

As I talked, he opened the door and slid into the passenger seat. "Start driving while you tell me more about Javier. I'll tell you where to turn." After just a few minutes, I was only a few feet down the road but far down the list of all that was "wrong" with Javier: "He's rude, disrespectful, mean . . ." Dr. Rhodes let me go on and on: ". . . disruptive, loud, and does not behave!" We were just a couple blocks from campus when he finally interrupted, "Pull into this driveway on the right."

I can remember every detail of what I saw that day. The property was littered with piles of trash, rusted cars, and dogs chained to trees. A pathway had been carved through the garbage that led to a structure that was part camper, part shanty. Blue tarps were draped over the top and a once-white shower curtain was rigged up to serve as the front door.

We sat there in silence as I stared at the kind of poverty I never knew existed. Finally, Dr. Rhodes said,

This is where Javier lives. When you consider all he has to deal with here at home, he ain't doing too bad at school. I want you to know that it's the kid who behaves the least who needs you the most.

31

It's OK to Say NO! Don't Overload!

Teachers are positive and helpful by nature. Many speak the language of affirmation. Since many teachers speak this language, it is hard for those teachers to say no. After all, you want to be seen as a team player, and you know that helping out now and then fosters a collegial and positive attitude in a school. Especially as a new teacher, you feel like you have to say yes to everything, so you may be the one people ask to cover a class, share materials, or serve on a committee. I remember during my first year teaching that I said yes to everything from coaching basketball and football to serving on the curriculum committee. It was a long, grueling year. After that year, I realized if I didn't learn to say no that I was going to burn out. After all, teacher attrition is around 10% to 15% a year, which is largely due to burnout. The ability to say no can help you prevent burnout. Never forget that time is our most precious resource and we only have a limited amount.

Saying no may not be easy or comfortable since we don't really like conflict, so it's easier to say yes. Here are a couple of strategies to help you say NO without feeling all the guilt often associated with it. You can be gracious and say "Thanks for asking me, but I just can't do that today," or "I'm so sorry, but I'm already on overload."

And if you are the type who just can't say the word NO, then simply say, "Thank you for considering me for this. Let me check my planner before I commit," or "I appreciate you asking me. I'm going to take time to fully consider this and I will let you know." Learning to say no will feel great, but remember that it's not that you don't care, it is a type of self-care. Balance is the key to happiness and longevity in teaching!

32

It's OK to Have a Bad Day!

I know administrators and even motivational speakers mean well, but sometimes they put too much pressure on teachers. You have heard them tell you that you may be the only positive influence in a child's life, so make sure you are positive all the time. I heard a comedian say it's important to be as positive as possible, but sometimes you just have a bad day. Sometimes you just want to go to Walmart and smack the smile off the greeter. While we would never do such a thing, we can relate to the sentiment because teaching is not an easy job.

We can relate to bad days and occasionally a bad week. I think the problem with many teachers is that we do work so hard and have a tendency to expect perfection from ourselves and that we always have to give our students our very best. But there are times when the cup is almost empty, or maybe you dropped the cup. It is just part of being a human. When those days happen, and they will, just realize that simply surviving is a victory!

I think the key to limiting the bad days is to reflect on them when you have them. Are you getting enough sleep, are you eating properly, or are you taking care of yourself? If these are the issues, then you definitely have control over these areas and can make change. If it is work related, then look for ways to help such as putting off grading assignments for a day or two and focus on taking care of yourself. The world won't end if everything isn't done at the end of the day. And when you do have that occasional bad day, remember the old saying, "**and it came to pass.**" Even when you have a bad day or are going through a tough situation, just know that it too will pass.

33

Be a Thermostat, Not a Thermometer

Whether you are in the classroom, the living room, or the board-room, always be the type of person who is a thermostat and not a thermometer. You may wonder what this has to do with teaching, but think about it like this; a thermometer is controlled by the environment, while a thermostat controls the environment. Do you control the environment of the classroom or do you let it control you?

I remember a couple of years ago when I was flying to Malaysia to speak at teaching centers throughout the country. We were about 10 hours into the flight, somewhere down the coast of Russia heading toward Japan, when we hit some major turbu-lence. It was the middle of the night, but I was awake, because I can't sleep on airplanes. I guess I feel like I need to be awake in case the pilots need me to help fly the plane or something. After a few bumps and quick drops, the pilot came over the speaker and requested the flight attendants to take a seat and buckle up immediately. You could see the fear on the flight attendants' faces as the they rushed to their seats, but what was interesting is that you couldn't hear the fear in the pilot's voice.

He continued to talk calmly to us as the plane was tossed around like a salad 30,000 feet in the air. The pilot talked us through what seemed like hours but was probably more like 10 minutes and in those few minutes I thought that it might be the end. After the plane settled and we cheered, I asked the flight attendant to let the pilot know we appreciated his calm under pressure. He created a climate of calmness in what could have been a chaotic situation. So, whether in the class or in life, be the thermostat, create a sense of calm instead of being influenced be the chaos.

34

Positively Positive!

I tweeted about being positive during negative times a few months ago and someone (who doesn't even follow me) replied that my tweet was toxic positivity. Toxic positivity? I wanted to reply and let this individual know what I thought of their toxicity, but I realized that would not be positive, so I just ignored them! But the reality is that it is important for us to have positive self-talk and to have a positive attitude, especially in the worst of times!

In fact, **positive** thinking and a **good attitude** help better our psychological well-being and help us cope better under stressful situations, such as at school. This doesn't mean you don't have bad days as mentioned before, but it means you don't let those days defeat you. That is why I think it is important for teachers and administrators to have a positive attitude. I used to say I never wanted a student when I was a teacher, or a teacher when I was an administrator, to leave school defeated or deflated. Positivity can be contagious.

We have always heard that a bad apple can spoil the whole bunch, but a little leaven causes the whole loaf of bread to rise. That leaven is the positivity we have every day. This metaphor can relate to your positivity improving or raising the attitudes of the people around you, but it can also mean your positivity affects or raises your overall health as well. Having a **positive** attitude has benefits such as lower blood pressure, less heart disease, **better** weight control, and less stress. Finally, having a positive attitude is like a magnet that will attract positive people to you. People who will keep you inspired and not defeated or deflated!

35

"Just a Teacher"

If there is one term that I hate to hear a teacher say it is, "I am just a teacher." Why do I dislike this term so much? Because it diminishes the value and importance of the role of a teacher. When I hear the term "just a teacher," I pause to think of "just" what a teacher does.

You work late into the evenings and weekends for no extra pay. You are constantly planning, grading, and preparing. And that is just one aspect of the job. You are also a counselor, confidante, nurse, and referee. You worry about your students like they were your own children. You are the students' role model for a love of learning. You are the one who believes in them, even when they don't believe in themselves. You are the one who gives hugs, when they need them and supplies, if they need them. You make every one of them feel like they are your favorite student and they are!

You help students build their dreams and their future. You are a compass for those who may have lost their way. You are a cheerleader to help them achieve their goals. Yes, you are a teacher, but you are not "just a teacher." You are an architect helping build the future one child at a time. Outside of their families, you are most likely the most important adult in many of their lives.

Remember the teachers who influenced your life? I bet you never thought of them as "just a teacher." And the students, whose lives you have influenced, will not remember you as "just a teacher." They will remember you as a person who gave them hope, who believed in them, and inspired them to dream! "Just a teacher?" Not hardly! You are a darn amazing, inspirational, affirmational, life-changing teacher!

36

You Have to Love Your Kids before You Can Love Your Kids

I would hear it from teachers all the time, "I seriously have no idea how you do it, Bowman. Every day they give you the worst kids in the district. Most of them have criminal records! How can you possibly love these kids?"

Honestly, I don't blame them a bit for asking. My students were a lot to handle. Many of them came to me as angry, hurt, disrespectful young people. So, I loved them.

My students despised anyone in an authority position and their attitudes and behaviors demonstrated that daily.

They yelled and they cursed. So, I loved them.

They were in emotional pain. So, I loved them.

They had been abandoned. So, I loved them.

They had been consistently disappointed and demoralized and dehumanized. So, I loved them.

My kids felt like they were broken. So, I loved them.

Let me be clear. When these kids showed up in my class, I didn't know them. I didn't like them. And, I certainly didn't love them. So, I loved them.

The emotion of loving students is created by the act of loving students.

Before you can love (n.) your students, you must love (v.) your students.

37

Teaching Is Not about Changing Kids; It's about Empowering Kids to Uncover the Greatest Version of Themselves

When my friend, Dr. Jeff Springer, was the principal at Magnolia High School, he could be heard spreading the VCL message throughout the halls every day. Day in and day out, year after year, he poured the VCL mantra into the hearts and minds of his students. Along with conversations, there were banners, t-shirts, caps, bracelets, hashtags, chants, cheers, and more. He desperately wanted his kids to know they were Valuable, Complete, and Loved.

All three tenants of the VCL message are critically important. However, it's that second one that I really find interesting: Complete.

When I first visited his campus, I asked Springer (pretty much everyone leaves off the Dr. Jeff part) what he meant when he told kids they're "complete." He said,

> We have over 2000 kids at Magnolia High School and we need every single kid to know that they were born perfectly complete. We need each of them to understand that they came into the world with a unique purpose along with the all the gifts and abilities needed to make the world a better place in their own individual way. As educators, it's not our job to change who they are;

but, instead, to empower them to uncover the greatest version of themselves so they can live up to who they're meant to be.

It's been four years since Springer repurposed from being a principal (He refuses to use the word retired). Today, Magnolia High School has a new principal along with a new theme, and I'm sure there are new banners, t-shirts, caps, chants, and cheers. However, if you do a quick search for #vcl on social media, you'll find that Springer is still spreading the gospel to the tens of thousands of students he's had over his 34 year career, as he continues to remind them that they are Valuable, Complete, and Loved.

38

Any Day of the School Year Can Become the New First Day of School

Just about every teacher I know goes through two phases of being an "Outstanding Teacher." The first phase happens at the beginning of the school year when you're rested, excited, and passionate about doing outstanding work with students in your classroom. The second phase of being an "Outstanding Teacher" typically happens somewhere in the middle of October when you find yourself exhausted, frustrated, and literally *out standing* in the hallway trying hold in the tears as you attempt to propel yourself through the classroom door.

Outstanding and *out standing* are two vastly different phases of teaching.

Phase Two is that point of physical and emotional exhaustion when we start thinking about what we're going to do different at the start the next grading period, or after the Holiday Break, or after Spring Break, or the beginning of the next school year. We tell ourselves, "Next year, I'm not going to have these problems because we're going start the year off differently by having crystal clear classroom expectations and procedures and I'm going to hold kids accountable from day one!" Or, some version of that.

One of the interesting differences between kids and adults is kids do not need a significant, landmark day to serve as a fresh, new beginning. Kids are so resilient that we really can create a brand new first day of school on any day of the school year. Simply let them know,

Kids, before we get started today, I want to remind you how much I love our classroom family. I dearly love each and every one of you. I spend more time here at school with you than I do my own family at home. The reason I want the best for us is because I care so much about you, our classroom family, and who we're becoming together. So, starting today – right now – here's what we're going to do differently…

There's no need to wait until you're deep into Phase Two of being an *out standing* teacher, crying in the hallway. You can start over at any point during Phase One so you can be exactly who your kids deserve throughout the school year – an outstanding teacher.

39

If You Don't Like Your Students, It's Because You Don't Know Your Students

Each year I coach thousands of educators on improving student behavior. In just about every session I'll inevitably hear some form of the statement: "Well, I have this one kid and he's absolutely terrible!"

I always immediately respond with, "Tell me why he's terrible." That's when they'll start going down the list. "He's rude, mean to other children, disobedient, defiant ..." I'll interrupt, "I'm not asking how he's terrible, I'm asking why he's terrible."

Silence.

I'll wait patiently. We'll sit in awkward silence. And, eventually the tension builds, and the response will typically be, "I don't know why he's terrible! He just is!"

Children are not "terrible." They may act terrible, but that doesn't mean they are terrible. For children, what they do isn't a reflection of who they are. We get tricked into thinking that behind every student misbehavior lies a negative character trait that leads to that behavior. That may be true for someone who is 60, but not for someone who's 6 or 16.

For kids, behind every act of student misbehavior lies an emotion that drives that behavior. Behind every student emotion is a consistent pattern of thought – an internal dialogue – that fuels that emotion. And, behind every consistent pattern of thought lies a mountain of stimulus – basically, everything a kid has ever experienced – that creates and influences those thoughts.

So, rather than focusing on the misbehavior, we have to influence that kid in such a way that we can affect his thought patterns, so that we shift his emotional state, so that we can transform how that kid behaves in the classroom.

The moment you position yourself as the most influential force in the life of a kid, is the moment that you'll be able to drastically impact, not just what that kid knows, but more importantly, a kid's behaviors, emotions, internal dialogue and, ultimately, who that kid is becoming.

40

Let's Not Settle for Accepting Differences; Let's Strive to Celebrate Differences

I was teaching at a high school in the suburbs of Houston that was in the midst of a dramatic demographic shift. Due to new construction of low-income and government housing, kids from Louisiana moving in after being displaced by Hurricane Katrina, and a host of other socio-economic factors, what once was an upper-middle class school transformed into a Title I, low-income campus filled with teens, many of whom were living in single parent, grandparent, and no parent homes immersed in poverty.

Creating a positive school culture was challenging. These kids did not grow up attending school together. They had no previous relationships in place. And, to be honest, they were not welcomed by many in the community. Yet overnight, they were thrown in to live together each day inside of an institutionalized building. One of the natural ways students were able to connect and develop relationships with each other was race, ethnicity, and nationality. In the hallways and in the cafeteria, the Black kids only hung out with the Black kids; the Mexican kids only hung out with the Mexican kids; and, the same was true for the Koreans, Guatemalans, Somalians, Salvadorians, Columbians, Pakistani, Egyptians, and the dozen or so other nationalities. Kids hung out with the kids they felt safe with and found commonalities and understanding.

The only time kids integrated was in the classroom, simply because they were forced to by proximity. As you can imagine, this made creating a strong, loving classroom family extremely challenging.

I remember attending a staff development session to address the issue with an "expert" in the field. She focused on the importance of kids learning to "accept" each other. That word – accept – made my skin crawl, and I could see that this was true for other teachers in attendance, as well. It just didn't feel right. As I squirmed in my seat, I finally looked up synonyms for accept and that's when I found the problem: tolerate, endure, put up with. I thought, "As educators, we're supposed to teach kids to tolerate and put up with other races, ethnicities, and nationalities? No thank you. Not in my classroom."

After talking with my students, they decided that they didn't want to be tolerated, instead, they wanted to be celebrated. Every day, without exception, we spent the first few minutes of class learning about each other. We had deep, open, uncensored conversations where the kids would search for the "weirdest" thing about each other's cultures (I tried to encourage them to use the word "unique," but they're kids. They stuck with weird. For them, they took pride in what others saw as weird). They loved asking each other, "What's the weirdest thing your family eats at the Holidays?" "What's the weirdest thing you do at church?" "What's the weirdest thing you have in your house?" It got to the point where every answer was followed with surprise, excitement, high-fives, and even deeper questions. Never before have I learned so much about how the beautiful uniqueness of humanity can connect all of us.

When you look up synonyms for celebrate, you'll find commemorate, rejoice, applaud, and revel. I think it's time that we all follow the lead of our students and consider celebrating each other rather than accepting each other.

41

Teaching Is a Team Effort!

Teaching may be one of the most isolating professions. Yes, you get to spend the day with your students, but there is often not a lot of interactions with colleagues. Teachers engage in less than 30 minutes of conversation each day with other teachers. Now, I know some of you may say, yes, I don't want to talk to anyone or I just want to be left alone during the few minutes I don't have students. And this is certainly understandable.

As an administrator, I always valued teamwork as much as a stellar teacher. That's because if greatness is performed in isolation, it does little to cultivate a dynamic school culture. But if you have a team of committed teachers to support, encourage, and motivate each other, that's a game changer! In fact, the best performing schools typically have the best functioning teams as well. This is because they are good at communicating, teamwork, and helping each other out. In poor performing schools, teachers often see asking for help as weak, feel they will be judged, or feel like others wouldn't do their fair share.

Administration should create an environment where teamwork is encouraged and the norm. But in any case, work to create the best team on your grade level and let it grow from there. It takes the whole team to be excellent. When you develop a team mindset, you exhibit:

- ♦ respect/trust for all members
- ♦ willing to share ideas/resources
- ♦ common goals/vision
- ♦ responsibilities based on strengths

- ◆ effective leadership
- ◆ everyone supported/valued
- ◆ see others as colleagues not competition

In education as in sports, it is not the best group of people who win, but the best team that wins!

42

Appreciation Is an Attitude, Not an Action!

If there is one thing we all have in common as humans, it is that we like to be recognized for a job well done. There is not much that makes your day more, even as a teacher, then when your administrator acknowledges your hard work, commitment, or going the extra mile for the school or students. And that just motivates us to want to do more for that type of leader. Well, students are no different. Students want to impress you and work hard for you. When you acknowledge that effort then they will seek to please you even more.

Appreciation is not just a pat on the back, but an ability to understand the worth, quality, or importance of something. So, value recognition as a frequent and ongoing activity that builds a strong, positive school culture. See recognition as a necessary ingredient and key driver of school success. Appreciation is shown through building a relationship based on trust, respect, and open communication. Think about it – if you appreciate someone in your personal life, such as a spouse, you don't just show it once. You show it consistently. The same is true of appreciating your students, but also your colleagues and even your administration. Remember everyone likes to be recognized for hard work. Students who feel valued and appreciated will work harder, be more engaged and are less likely to be disruptive and off task. Finally, appreciation by definition means to add value to something. As teachers, we should be adding value to the lives of those we teach and work alongside. So don't just say you appreciate, but show appreciation for others and I hope others show you the appreciation that you deserve. And I hope you know that the authors of this book appreciate you for all you do for your kids!

43

Challenge the Process

As an administrator, I loved having strong teachers who weren't afraid to speak up. Now, I am not talking about the one or two who complain about everything. You know, the ones who hate hot coffee and cold ice cream. They are never satisfied!

But the teachers I am talking about are the ones who are passionate about their work and their students. They are always looking for the best way to do things and what is best for the students. Strong leaders love strong teachers because iron sharpens iron and good leaders know strong teachers will only make them better. If you have a weak administrator, then they are usually afraid of strong teachers and they see feedback or input as a personal attack on them.

However, challenging the process really shows that you have a healthy team culture, where people feel free to speak up and discuss different strategies or plans to be successful. It can improve the status quo, help create innovative solutions, build stronger confidence in implementing ideas, and build stronger relationships on team.

Here are three keys that make the process most successful:

Focus on being proactive and not reactive means you think through the issue and not just react to it.

Focus on relating and not on being right means you seek to find the best resolution and not just your resolution.

Focus on the issue and not on the individual means that you don't let personalities or ego get in the way. It is about the issue(s) not on whether or not you like the person with whom you disagree. So don't take the disagreement personally.

44

Bringing Out the Best in Students

Did you know that educate comes from the root word *Educere*, which means to lead or draw out. We have always heard education is the filling of a bucket or even a lighting of a fire, but in reality education means to bring out the best in students. What is their best? It is their strengths and passions.

If we focus mainly on students' weaknesses, they will probably spend their life fearing failure because that is all that was focused on in school. Instead, we need to focus on their strengths, abilities, and passions to experience success, which builds confidence. When a student gains confidence, they will be willing to take risks and fail because they have experienced precious success.

The reason we tend to focus on weaknesses in education is that we as teachers are often faced with the issue. I remember my first year teaching and how excited I was to bring my strengths to the classroom. The only problem was my administration wanted me to focus on a PAC, which is basically picking two areas of weakness and focusing on them. When we focus on our weaknesses we may become incrementally better, but when we focus on developing our strengths then we become exponentially more successful. Let's change the focus in the classroom and help students realize their full potential. Because every student has unique talents that can help them succeed in school and life. Help them discover and build on those talents and you will have changed their lives for the better!

45

Lace up Your Shoes

Coach John Wooden was probably the greatest basketball coach of all time. He was able to recruit the best basketball players in the country to play for him. What is interesting is that even though he had some of the most amazing athletes, he always started with the basics. Now some may think the basics are dribbling or shooting, but that is not where he started. The first thing he taught his world class recruits was how to put on their socks and lace up their shoes. Why did he start there? Because he knew if socks aren't put on properly, then you can get blisters, which can affect everything you do.

So, when you have high expectations of your students, children, spouses, or even colleagues, remember that for them to truly excel, you have to provide the support and tools they need to be successful. And sometimes it is the simple things in the process that may make all the difference. And never forget the important of properly lacing your shoes!

But this is also to inspire you to never forget the little things in your pursuit of excellence. You may not have the position you want yet, or achieved all that you desire, but that doesn't mean you won't get there. I heard a military commander speak several years ago and he said the first thing to do every day is make you bed. He said excellence is a process that starts with discipline and consistency. And he said if you do happen to have a bad day, at least you have a well-made bed to fall into when you get home. So, whatever your pursuit of excellence might happen to be, don't forget to lace up first!

46

Be the Teacher Your Kids Need, Deserve, and Will Remember Forever

As I watch adults go about their everyday lives, I wonder what their experience was like back when they were in school. I wonder if they felt like they were successful, if they can recall the details of the classroom, or if they loved or hated school.

I wonder if they remember their teachers.

So, a couple of years ago, I decided to start asking people. One day in the grocery store, I took out my phone, turned on my camera, and clicked Record Video. I walked up to a lady, I gently put my hand on her shoulder, I held up my camera to record, and (in my most animated elementary teacher tone of voice) I said, "Hi. Let's record a quick video. I'm going to ask you about your teachers from when you were in school." With a big smile, she, said, "Great!" So, I continued, "Think back to when you were in school. Of all the teachers you had, who comes to mind first as the one who made the biggest difference in your life?"

Not only could she remember the teachers name, grade, and school, but she was excited to describe every aspect of the experience. Even after 40 years, her detailed recollection was mind-boggling. So, I decided to ask another person, and then another, and then another.

Since that day, I've recorded hundreds of videos of ordinary people who love talking about their extraordinary teachers. And, here's what I've discovered is true for everyone I've interviewed: Without exception, people don't remember academic lessons, they remember life lessons. They don't remember classroom rules, they remember classroom relationships. The don't remember worksheets and assessments, they remember experiences. When they got in trouble, they don't remember consequences, they remember conversations. And, they don't remember what they learned, they remember feeling loved.

Be the teacher your kids need, deserve, and will remember for the rest of their lives.

47

What's the Real Lesson of Your Classroom? The One Your Kids Can't Google the Answer To?

I remember reading about Dr. B. F. Skinner in one of my undergraduate teacher preparation courses. He wrote, "Education is what survives when what has been learned has been forgotten" (*New Scientist*, May 21, 1964). When I first read that, it really didn't sink in. A lot in that class didn't sink in for me. I think had a lot to do with the fact that I was still a teenager and had yet to spend a single day in an actual classroom teaching real kids.

But, I do remember the day that quote first made sense to me. About five years into my career, I was teaching high school biology and during a department meeting I was discussing how frustrated I was that my students seemed to understand the material during class, but their test grades were terrible. I was agonizing over what I could do different, what I could do better. Lots of suggestions and ideas were shared from everyone – except Mr. Zucker. He just sat in his chair, leaning back against the wall, patiently waiting for us to finish. Zucker never really said much of anything to anyone.

Late that afternoon, as I was cleaning up my classroom and preparing to leave, Zucker peeked his head into my classroom and said, "Hey man. The kids are going to forget all the stuff. You get that, right?"

I said, "What? Who's going to forget what stuff?"

That's when he explained Dr. Skinner's quote:

Your kids are going to forget all the biology information you are trying to stuff into their brains during class.
They're not going to retain any of it. Even if they all made
100s on the final exam, they wouldn't be able to pass
that same test just a few weeks later. So, as you're trying
to figure out how to help them do better on academic
assessments, you should also spend some time thinking
about the question, "What's the real lesson of your classroom?" Teaching school – especially high school kids –
is all about using the content of your classroom as the
vehicle to teach the lessons that will impact who they are
and who they're becoming.

I think if Dr. Skinner were alive today, he might want us to
spend some time thinking about and answering the question,
"Your students have access to 100% of your content on their cell
phones. What's the one lesson that they can't find on Google that
you want your kids to remember for the rest of their lives?"

48

Of Course He Behaves That Way, Acts Like That, and Does Those Things; That's Why He's in Your Class, He Needs You

With a big a smile and sincere excitement, I said, "Welcome to our class Jeremiah! We're all so glad you're joining our class!"

"Don't you ever say my name! Keep my name out your mouth!"

Those were Jeremiah's first 12 words to me the moment we met on his first day he joined our class. After which, he then leaned against the wall, right by the door, refusing to sit down as he scowled at me for the entire class period.

As soon as class was over, I literally sprinted down the hallway with Jeremiah's schedule in hand to the counselor's office. I barged into her office and immediately started pleading my case. Frantically, I begged,

Please don't do this to me! Why did you put that kid in my class? You have to change his schedule! I'm begging you not to do this to me! I have 34 kids in that class, he makes 35! No one else has more than 23 during that same class period! Why are you doing this to me? You have to move that kid!

The school counselor calmly looked up at me over her reading glasses and quietly said, "Bowman, I could have put him with any of those other teachers. But, he doesn't need those teachers. He needs you."

I sat down. I took a deep breath. And, I thought about Jeremiah. After just a few minutes, I knew exactly what to do.

I left the office and found Jeremiah in his next class leaning against the wall, right by the door, scowling at his teacher. I whispered to him through the open door, "Hey man, sneak out into the hallway when your teacher's not looking." He timed it perfectly and stepped into the hallway. It was clear Jeremiah had some experience sneaking out of class. I said,

> Listen, our class has 35 kids in it. All the other classes at that time have less than 23. If anyone tries to move you out of our class, do not let them. In fact, if you ever get called down to the office for anything, you come see me first. We'll handle it together. I got you. You're not going anywhere; you're staying with me. Cool?

It was obvious that he was suspicious as he stared at me for a long time. Finally, he whispered back, "Cool."

I thought this was a good time to push the boundaries just a little bit, "Ok, great. See you tomorrow … 'J.'" His head snapped around, he scrunched up his face and glared at me. I smiled at him and explained, "Hey brother, that's not your name in my mouth, that's just the first letter in my mouth." I continued smiling big as he continued to give me the death stare.

He didn't smile back that day, but I could tell he was fighting it. Progress.

49

If You Own 100% of It, You Can Affect 100% of It

One common trait among those teachers who are the happiest and most satisfied is that they honestly believe that whatever happens in their classrooms is all their fault – 100% of it, both the good and the bad.

When you first consider this belief system, not only does it seem counterintuitive, but it also feels like it's a lot of pressure and responsibility – and, yes, it is. However, the happiness and contentment we're all searching for lies within the act of taking total responsibility.

So much of the emotional stress and anxiety in teaching is the result of feeling like you're not able to control the variables. Think about all that you've heard in a typical teacher gripe sessions:

> I get no support from the administration ... these kids are disrespectful ... their parents didn't raise them right ... their previous teachers didn't adequately prepare them ... the curriculum is terrible ... and, the copy machine is broken, AGAIN!

Regardless of whether any of that is true or not, the real stress lies in that if it is true, you cannot affect any of it. That sense of powerlessness leads to stress and anxiety.

There's only one thing you can affect and it's the only thing that truly matters: Accepting the fact that you are the single most important determining factor in the achievement of students while taking total responsibility for everything that happens in your classroom as you focus 100% on your ability to lead and teach your classroom family no matter the circumstances.

I know, that seems like a lot. But it's truly where you'll find the most happiness, satisfaction, and contentment. The moment you own 100% of what happens in your classroom is the moment you can affect 100% of what happens in your classroom.

One of my favorite teachers has a saying, "When it's all amazing, it's because I'm amazing. When it all sucks, it's because I suck." She takes total ownership and she's also one of the happiest and most satisfied teachers I know.

50

Just in Case You Don't Believe Me about Taking 100% Ownership in Your Classroom, Let's Quantify Influence, That Always Helps

The conversation starts as it usually does, with the teacher stating, "I don't think you understand what it's like trying to teach these kids in this school. It's just not possible."

As always, I begin by asking, "Specifically, what makes teaching these kids impossible?" Without taking a breath (or including commas or periods), he launches into his answer:

> We have the worst principal ever and the kids are poor and don't care and their parents—if they have any— don't care and we get no support from the community and there's absolutely no funding and we have no technology and the curriculum is garbage and …

"Whoa!" I interrupt.

> Hang on a second and take a breath. Let's quantify each of the challenges so we know exactly what we're working with and what we can affect. Let's start with your principal. What percentage of the problem is your principal when it concerns what specifically happens in your classroom?

After thinking for a moment, he answers, "She's at least 25% of the problem, and I'm being nice."

"Ok, I got it." Next, I ask, "Tell me about the attitudes of your kids and their parents. What percentage of the problem is that?"

He answers, "Their attitudes are a huge problem! That's at least 40%."

I let him know that I'm keeping up, "25% is the principal and 40% is the kids and their parents. Now, talk to me about the community. As far as affecting specifically what happens in your classroom, what percentage of the problem is the community?"

He answers, "Definitely less, maybe 10%."

I reassure him, "I understand. We're at 25, 40, and 10, for a total of 75%. Tell me about funding and technology."

"We have none of either!" He estimates, "At least 10% each."

It's time for me to lay it all out so he can clearly see the picture he just painted.

We're already at 95% and we haven't even got to the garbage curriculum. And, you're telling me that you can't control any of those circumstances. If you could only affect the remaining 5% of what happens in your classroom, why would anyone even try?

Please remember, you are 100% the single most important determining factor for academic and personal success in the classroom. We must make the difficult decision to own 100% of everything that happens in our classrooms.

If you own 100% of what happens, you can affect 100% of what happens.

51

Teacher of the Year Awards

Teaching is one of the most isolating jobs as we all know. Some days it seems like it is just you on your island with your students like an episode of *Survivor*! We also know that you can have bad days, or may simply be exhausted. This is when you may need some affirmation yourself. We know most teachers speak the language of affirmation, but sometimes you need it spoken to you. And there is no better affirmation than the drawings and notes from your students.

So, I learned early in my career to keep all the drawings and notes that my students made for me and to keep them handy to pull out and look through when I was having a bad day. As I reflect over my career, some of my most treasured memories from teaching are the notes and drawings that students left on my desk or drew on the board. Now of course I enjoyed some of the great gifts that I was given over the years, but those were given out of appreciation; the notes and drawings were given out of love. They are the way young students try to express their gratitude and love for you.

I remember near the end of my first year that my students had created a booklet for me that had drawings and letters made by them. I had already kept all the ones they had made for me through the year, but this was extra special. Even though it's been over 25 years, I remember like it was yesterday. But, it made me realize early in my career that we don't just teach a subject but that we teach students, students who look to you for support, encouragement, and validation. Your impact may be greater than you ever know. So, on those tough days, pull out a note or a drawing, and remember your why! There's no better pick me up! These are the real Teacher of the Year Awards!

52

Every Day Is a New Beginning

One of the most effective teaching strategies is to let every day be a fresh new start. This is important for you and for your students, especially if yesterday was an off or bad day. Now, I could probably have titled this "letting things go," because it is really the same mindset. But the idea is that students will make poor choices or have bad days but that doesn't mean they can't move on from them.

Have you ever had a student who acted out or just seemed frustrated, but it was out of character for them? Some of them worry about whether or not you will still like them. One of the first things I would tell students at the beginning of the year was that I have high expectations, but that I don't take it personal if you don't always live up to them. You may have consequences to an action, but every day is a new day in the classroom. Now imagine how comforting that can be to some students just to know you aren't going to take things personal?

I am glad that life is that way for us as adults as well. There were days as a teacher, administrator, and even now when I just fail miserably. There are days when I just want to go home, fall into bed, and pretend the day never happened. And there are some days I do, we all do, so yes it is normal that you feel that way as well. Fortunately, we get to start every day new as well. Always be forward focused on new goals, new hopes, and dreams. And give yourself a little grace and don't hold grudges against yourself for not always being perfect. Learn to let some things go, and realize every day is a new beginning!

53

You Inc!

Have you ever wondered why your school has a mission statement? Or why you have to meet and discuss it every year? The purpose is to have a roadmap toward goals that help fulfill the purpose of the school. If mission statements are important for schools and businesses, then shouldn't we have them for our own lives? A personal mission statement can help you identify your values and goals, defining what matters most to you professionally or even personally, and help you define a path to fulfilling your purpose. Now hopefully it is not like many school mission statements that hang on the wall and are never given much attention throughout the year.

When I speak to young people, one of my points is to help them think of themselves as a business. Think about it, if you are a business, then what is the purpose of the business? What is your purpose? How do you know if you are achieving your purpose without a set of goals to help you?

Some examples of mission statements include, "To encourage, engage, and equip others to believe in themselves." "To positively impact the life of every person I teach." "To encourage everyone I interact with on a daily basis." And, of course, my personal mission statement: "To help educators maximize their talents professionally and personally to reach their full potential!".

So have goals: Daily, weekly, short-term, and long-term goals that help guide your mission and help you live out your purpose. I have interviewed some of the most successful leaders in every industry and one characteristic they all shared is that they set daily, weekly, and long term goals. They knew to succeed that they needed to have a plan for success. When you think of life in this manner, you will live not just like a person with a mission, but like a person on a mission! Setting goals and crushing them!

54

Know Your Worth?

While it has become almost cliché for people to say in our culture, it really is important for you know your worth! The reason it has a question mark here is because when is the last time you thought about your worth? Especially as a teacher, you get caught up in the busyness of the day, and often you may not give much thought to what you are contributing to your classroom, school, and society in general.

Another reason we don't reflect on our worth is that our culture and even education is so focused on weaknesses. As teachers, when you are evaluated the focus is often on areas of improvement, or administrators try to sugar coat it by calling them areas of growth. We do the same with students when we focus on areas in which they need to improve instead of on areas in which they do well. If we as a society and an educational system focused more on our talents instead of weaknesses, we would all feel more valuable.

In fact, the term *talent* was originally a measure of currency in ancient times. Some estimate the value to be around $1.4 million by today's standards. You are a million dollar woman or a million dollar man! This is also why it's so important to be yourself. I have often said that I can walk into five different classrooms and see five different teachers teaching five different ways and they all make an impact. You have talents and abilities that are unique to you and which make you an amazing teacher and human! So, get up, look in the mirror, and tell yourself that you are priceless and then go make this day amazing!

55

Your Purpose Is Greater Than Your Struggle

I think one of the most frustrating parts of teaching is that you impact lives every year, but then the students move on to the next grade, or school, or district and you lose touch. Even the ones who are greatly impacted by you may not ever let you know. So it seems like a thankless job sometimes. And then you have days when you struggle and wonder if you are making a difference at all.

Those are tough days when you question if you are doing your best, or if it even matters, or if anyone even cares. Am I making a difference? Is it worth the struggle? I think every teacher has asked those questions. Well, you do make a difference, even on the days you don't feel like it. Don't ever feel like you aren't being effective during the times that you struggle or have difficulty. Your purpose is greater than your struggles. A perfect example would be one of your students who has been struggling with a concept or a subject, and it is just a constant struggle to help them understand, but one day he finally gets it.

You will also have many students through the years who are struggling with issues that you may not even know about, but still seek daily to inspire them, believe in them, and make a difference in their lives. Your purpose isn't just educating the student, but helping them realize their potential. In essence, you are giving them hope that they can succeed in life and that is a purpose worth any amount of struggle. There's a reason so many of you feel like your job is a calling, and it's important to keep in mind during the rough times, So, don't give up, don't get too down, and know that even on your worst day, you can still make a difference in the lives of your students and that should be motivation to keep you going!

56

No More Excuses!

I remember working with a teacher who seemed to be late every day. No, the teacher wasn't me, but it was a male teacher. What was most irritating is that he always had an excuse for being late. Traffic was bad, there was an accident, and the list goes on and on and on. In fact, he seemed to think that as long as he had a good excuse that it was okay to be continually late.

While we may not use excuses on a consistent basis, we are guilty of making excuses from time to time. And just like this teacher, we feel like if it is a good excuse then everything is okay. However, even the best excuses are still just excuses and keep us from accomplishing our goals. How often do you put off things like going back to school, trying for a new position, or pursuing a passion by coming up with as many excuses as possible for not doing them?

And the sad part is that if we come up with good enough excuses then we feel better about not pursuing those goals or passions. So, I say, no more excuses! I often use the illustration of exercising when I talk about no more excuses, because I think we can all relate to it. I know many adults who tell me they just don't have time to exercise, but these same people will watch an hour or two hours of television every night. In fact, did you know the average adult watches over five hours of television each day? Now I know that's not the average teacher, but you have to learn to find time for what is important to you.

So, make up your mind that you are not going to make excuses anymore, but you are going to pursue the goals and interests that you have been putting off for months or even years. Make a plan, set goals, and then accept no more excuses. Remember, even the best excuse is still an excuse to keep you from reaching your fullest potential!

57

Don't Just Lean in but Lean On!

A common phrase in education now is to "lean in." Administrators often use this phrase to encourage teachers to lean into problems, difficulties, and issues. I think it is important for us to persevere and to try harder when things get tough, because it not only helps us become more successful, but it is important for students to see how we work harder when we struggle as well.

But overcoming obstacles is not just about self-will; it is about encouragement and team effort too. So, don't just lean into the tough times this year, but lean on each other in the tough times. I often use the analogy of geese flying to reinforce team concepts. So think of what happens when a goose becomes fatigued, sick or is injured. The goose has to land to recover, but what is interesting is that he isn't left alone. When this occurs, two geese will stay back with the goose until it is able to fly again.

Why do two geese stay back? They stay to help protect the goose until it is healthier, and when they do return to the flock, it is much easier and efficient if they are flying in the "V" formation than if the goose is flying alone. This allows them to return to their team more quickly and efficiently. The takeaway here is when you are struggling, don't feel like you have to do it all alone. Yes, lean in and do what you can, but make sure you are surrounded by a team who is willing to shoulder the load with you, and when they are struggling, make sure you help them shoulder their load. Imagine how much more effective we would all be if we learned to lean on each other when dealing with difficulties. This is true in our professional and personal lives.

58

Honk If You . . .

Don't you love all the bumper stickers that say "honk if you love . . . ?" The subjects vary from Jesus, cats, honking, cheese, to terms I can't write in this book. What's even more humorous is that if someone were to honk at the bumper sticker, it would make the person angry if they'd forgotten it was there.

But the honking I am referring to is not for bumper stickers, but for the encouragement given by geese in flight. Have you ever wondered why you can hear a team of geese honking when they are flying through the air (and yes, they are called a team in flight)? The reason they honk is to encourage those up front to keep up their speed. When a goose falls out of formation, it suddenly feels the drag and resistance of trying to go it alone and quickly gets back into formation to take advantage of the lifting power of the team. The beauty of the team is that no matter which goose is out in the lead they are supporting and encouraging it until it tires, and then another one will take the heavy load.

While you would think we would work better as a team than a gaggle of geese, it seems we often have a hard time doing so in schools. But what if administrators and teachers all supported and encouraged each other? When is the last time you verbally encouraged colleagues or, better yet, when is the last time you encouraged your leaders? Don't be afraid to speak up and speak out to let others know you appreciate them and to encourage them. Hopefully your team is working toward the same goals and a little honking may be just what they need to keep going strong!

59

Utilizing the Pygmalion Effect

Do you remember the musical *My Fair Lady*? It was based upon the play *Pygmalion*, in which professor Henry Higgins turns a common cockneygirl, Eliza Doolittle, into a sophisticated lady. While these are works of fiction, the Pygmalion effect is actually a psychological phenomenon known as a self-fulfilling prophecy.

Basically what it means is that students will live up to whatever expectations you have for them. Have you ever had a teacher tell you that a student you are getting in the fall is a poor student or causes a lot of trouble? This sets up a situation where you will probably expect this behavior, and you may treat them differently, even if unconsciously. But if you think a student is smart, then there is a greater chance she will perform at a higher level regardless of her intelligence.

Remember this when you interact with your students, or even your children, family, or friends. If you don't think a person can achieve a high level of success then they probably won't. What is interesting is this doesn't necessarily mean that they aren't capable, but that you may not be using your best leadership skills when helping them because you don't expect them to excel. So, don't write off any students, but expect the best from them and see what a difference it makes.

As a teacher, I wanted every one of my students to think they were amazing in science. When they moved to the next grade, I would tell teachers how fortunate they were to be getting this group of students. More often than not, the students lived up to the expectations and the teachers would treat them the same way too.

Try this with yourself as well. We often expect that things won't go as planned or that we won't do something well, but what if you believe in yourself and have high expectations of yourself? I believe that people live up to our lowest expectations, so have high expectations for your students and for yourself. Now go do great things!

60

Let Your Classroom Be the Incubator of Character, Potential, and Self-Esteem

During a visit to an elementary school, I was walking through the work room as a group of third grade teachers were having lunch. I overheard one teacher exclaim, "That kid is just so lazy!" Another chimed in, "And irresponsible! He never brings a thing to class." Another, "Well, it doesn't matter what he brings to class, he's not going to do anything anyway." The next, chomping on a mouth full of cheese crackers, "And he's so rude!"

I hear negative conversations among educators where children are disparaged and criticized a lot with the statement, "That kid is so _____." I think we underestimate the damage that is done with those defining statements about children.

I understand and agree that, at times, teaching can be an incredibly difficult, exhausting, and emotionally painful. And sometimes you just have to vent your frustrations. But, I'm not sure there is a more reckless and dangerous negative statement than, "That kid is so _____."

It's a statement that permanently tattoos a defining label onto a kid's personality for everyone to read. That label now lets every teacher know, "This is who I am, and this is what you should expect of me."

Worse, that label lets the child know, "This is who I am, and this is the expectation I should live up to."

Let me be clear. A third grader is not lazy, or irresponsible, or rude. Yes, a child may act like that, but that's not who he is. The same is true for all kids whether they're 8 years old, or in the 8th grade, or 18 years old. They're all just simply children who are inside the four walls of the incubator of character, potential, and self-esteem – your classroom.

61

Why Would a Kid Want to Be Successful if He Doesn't Remember What Success Feels Like?

You know that kid in your class who requires all kinds of special precautions because he has crazy food allergies? He's allergic to peanuts, tree nuts, chocolate, shellfish, eggs, milk, and who knows what else. He's the one whose mom emails you monthly just to make sure the epinephrine auto-injectors she's installed in your classroom are not expired.

Well, I was that kid.

As a child, I would attend birthday parties and just sit quietly and watch as the other children would frantically shovel mountains of cake and ice cream into their faces. At school, I would see the excitement as kids would eat smuggled contraband candy bars on the playground. When a mom would bring donuts to our class, my classmates would jump up and down and cheer as they were passed out – skipping me, of course.

"Hal'ergy" would just sit quietly and watch.

Today, as an adult, not much has changed. When the P.T.O. brings brownies to school, teachers race to the office. The academic teachers attempt to devour them all before the fine arts teachers find out about them. I once witnessed two feisty Language Arts teachers almost get into fist fight over who gets the corner brownie. Apparently, those are the most coveted brownies. I wouldn't know.

I just sit quietly and watch.

Knowing about my allergies, teachers always say, "I feel so sorry for you! Oh my God, these are so delicious! I have been craving these brownies! I can't imagine how terrible it must be for you not to be able to eat these!"

I have always thought it was interesting that people assumed I felt like I was missing out on something I have never experienced. How could I miss what I've never had? How could I possibly want what I've never had?

Now, think about the kids in your classroom who struggle academically. For some, it has literally been years since they have felt what it's like to be successful in school. For a few, they've never felt what academic success feels like. Not once have they ever experienced that euphoric rush of dopamine and endorphins that occurs with accomplishment in the classroom.

It's no wonder why some kids don't have a desire to be successful in school. You can't crave what you've never experienced. I have never experienced a brownie, so I don't crave a brownie. Our struggling students who have never experienced academic success, don't crave academic success. So, before we raise academic expectations and increase rigor and demand more from our kids, let's first set them up with academic success so they know what it feels like. That's the only way they could ever begin to crave it.

62

Psssst I Have a Secret to Tell You: That Boy Who Acts Like He Doesn't Care About Anything Is an Amazing Actor

I'm going to speak on behalf of boys. Not all boys, of course. But what I'm about to tell you applies to lots of boys. Probably more than you would ever imagine.

Granted, this is not scientific research. There were no samplings of random populations and I don't have peer-reviewed, published data. This is based on my personal experience, as well as conversations with hundreds of young men in their late teens and early twenties and even deeper discussions with men in their later years of adulthood.

When boys are young, in their early years of elementary school, they have the ability to freely express their emotions with congruency. At that age, what you see is what you get. When a boy appears to be excited, he's probably excited. When he appears to be sad, he's generally sad. When he looks mad, he feels mad. Pretty simple.

But, as boys grow older, typically right before puberty, things become a lot more emotionally complicated (Get ready, here comes my completely unscientific theory). At this age, there's a shift in the way many boys process positive emotions. When they feel an emotion that moves them in a positive way, in a way that feels good – they try to stop it. Once they realize they can't stop it, or even control it, they will resort to disguising how they feel with the opposite emotion.

You might see an example of this during an awe-inspiring fireworks display. A boy will act unimpressed as he says, "Who cares!" At the end of an emotionally moving movie as everyone around him is tearing up, overwhelmed with deep feelings of joy, you might hear, "This is stupid." Or, during an exciting activity, the boy will state, "This is boring."

As a teacher, you'll certainly run into this in every class, with every age of boy. As you inspire and encourage your students, you'll have boys who will act indifferent. As you celebrate your students, some boys will act irritated. As you express how much you truly care for your students, some boys will answer with an eye-roll and a slow shake of the head.

Please remember, this is an act. It's a disguise. Your efforts are absolutely working. The messages are being received and they're making a difference. No matter how convincing the act, I can confidently assure you that your boys are feeling those emotions. In fact, they're often feeling those emotions more intensely than anyone else in the classroom. But for some reason, they just can't get themselves to express it right now.

Please don't give up on your boys. I promise you: Everything you're doing is working. I know for a fact it is. Your boys are definitely feeling those emotions. I know for a fact they are. All of your effort matters. I know for a fact it does.

How can I be so sure? I was that boy.

63

Greeting Kids at the Door Is the Most Important Moment of the Educational Process

Over the years it has become obvious that our most effective teachers are also the happiest. They are those teachers who have developed a sense of personal and professional satisfaction through teaching. Simply put, they love teaching. And, it's no secret what sets them apart. They have deepest desire and the greatest aptitude for building meaningful relationships with their students.

When it comes to the art of building relationships with kids, I believe we get too caught up in the psychological details of WHY it's important, and the complexities of HOW it's done. Rather than the "Why" and the "How," sometimes all that matters is the WHAT.

When educators ask me, "WHAT can I do to start building more meaningful relationships with the students in my classroom?" My answer is always the same: Greet and connect with every single kid – physically, verbally, and emotionally – as they enter your classroom, every single day, without exception.

Teachers typically don't say it out loud, but I can always see them responding to my answer in their minds, "All of that? Every kid? Every day? I don't have that kind of time! You're crazy!"

Of course, in my head I'm replying, "Yes, all of that. Yes, every kid. Yes, every day. Yes, you do. Yes, maybe a little."

I understand that it may seem like a huge time investment. But, I promise you, it's not.

Here comes Jessica walking down the hall toward me. As soon as I finish greeting the kid I'm currently engaged with, I enthusiastically call out, "JESSICA!" As she's walking towards me, she looks up, we make eye contact as she sees a giant smile with my eyes wide open and my eyebrows arched as high as possible. She immediately replies in kind with an excited, "BOWMAN!" I put my fist up because I know she prefers the "bump" rather than a handshake, high five, or hug. As we fist bump, I deepen the eye contact. Because of how she has already responded, along with her body language, I know I don't need to check in with her. She's clearly her normal, happy self today. So, instead of the typical "How are you today?" I give her a fun directive to generate a positive emotion, "Tell me how amazing youth group was last night!" (I know that she doesn't ever miss youth group on Wednesday nights). She says, "Super amazing!" As she enters through the classroom door, I finish with, "Awesome. Welcome home." And, I'm onto the next kid.

Still think it's too time intensive? Use the stopwatch on your phone and time me. Without all the play-by-play commentary, it goes like this:

"JESSICA!"
"BOWMAN!"
* Bump *
"Tell me how amazing youth group was last night!"
"Super amazing!"
"Awesome. Welcome home."

A lot happened inside of those five seconds. I was able to connect with Jessica physically, verbally, and emotionally. I deepened our relationship. I set the tone for the class period. And, it didn't interrupt the flow of kids into the classroom.

For the casual, non-educator observer, that interaction with Jessica might not seem like much. But, great teachers know that over the course of a school year those moments add up, multiply, and compound into the building blocks of a relationship that will last forever.

64

It's OK to Find Out about a Kid's Past; Not to Lower Expectations for That Kid, but Instead, to Better Understand How to Teach and Love That Kid

When I was a young teacher, I remember getting my class roster a few days before the kids showed up for the first day of school. I can recall all the teachers huddled up, pouring over their lists of students, and talking about the kids in their classes for the new school year. I heard a teacher tell her colleague about a second grader, "You have to stay on top of that one! Don't give him an inch." An assistant principal said to a teacher about a 4th grader, "You send me that girl anytime you need to. I'll put her in her place." I heard another teacher, "He's back? He's in the 5th grade AGAIN? Good luck with him. I almost retired because of that one!"

My mentor teacher grabbed me by my arm and pulled me into the hallway. She closed the door behind her and said,

Do not listen to those teachers. When you get your class roster at the beginning of each year, I want you to immediately put it in a file so no one can see it. Then, walk out of that room so you don't have to listen to any of that.

I agreed with her. "Yes, Ma'am. I understand. It's a new year and every kid deserves a new start with a blank slate, right?" I asked.

"Well, you're close." She said,

Yes, every kid deserves a fresh start, not just every year, but every day, as well. But, there's more to it than that. Always remember this: It's ok to find out about a kid's past, not to set academic or behavioral expectations, but instead so you can learn how they need to be taught and how they need to be loved.

I nodded, "Ok, I got it."

As we stood in the hallway, we could both hear teachers complaining about their kids on the other side of the door. She said, "Please don't ever participate in what's happening in that room."

The door suddenly opened into the hallway and a teacher walked out. "Mr. Bowman!" she called out as she began to laugh. "I heard that you have Jackson in your class this year! Let me tell you about that one!" as she continued laughing.

Immediately I said, "No thank you. I'd rather be surprised."

Still laughing, "Oh, you're going to be surprised alright!" as she continued walking down the hall.

I looked at my mentor teacher and she put her finger up to her mouth as if to say, "Shhh, don't say another word. Don't engage with her." Then she whispered to me, "No. SHE is the one who's going to be surprised by the work you do Jackson."

65

If You're Going to Make a Difference, You Must Be Different

I've always said that it's impossible to judge a student's academic potential by their appearance. And, I still believe it to this day. At this point in my career I have hundreds of examples of how that statement has proven to be true; students who I thought would do incredibly well, ended up struggling, and those who I thought would struggle, ended up doing incredibly well. Just like the saying goes, "You can't judge a book by its cover."

However, if there is one thing you can accurately determine about a kid just by looking at them, it's whether or not a kid feels successful in school and has enjoyed their time thus far. With only a split-second glance from a mile away, you can tell whether a kid likes school and wants to be there.

You can witness crystal clear examples of this every year on the first day of school as kids are walking to their first class. Lots of kids are smiling and talking and looking around, taking it all in as they're filled with excited anticipation to kick off another school year. A few kids, however, walk slowly, silently, with their heads down as they prepare to endure another school year filled with feelings of embarrassment, confusion, and failure. Of course, they're dreading this moment. Why wouldn't they be? After enduring the same experiences, the same results, and the same painful emotions year after year, why would those kids be filled with anything other than dread?

On day one of the school year, if a kid who has struggled and has been unsuccessful for years walks into your class and you teach them just like every teacher has taught them for the last five years, can you expect anything different from that kid? If that kid walks into your class and you assess them just like every teacher has assessed them for the last five years, should you expect anything different from that kid? If that kid walks into your class and you greet them the same, talk to them the same, sit them into the same typical seating chart, gesture the same, call on them the same, look at them the same, prepare them the same, and set the same expectations for them as every teacher has for the last five years, do you really have the right to expect anything different other than them replicating exactly the same results they have produced for the last five years?

Of course not.

I know it sounds cliché, almost as bad as that back-to-school teacher t-shirt you saw on Instagram, but it's so profoundly true: If you're going to make a difference, you must be different.

If you're wondering, being the educator who's different for that kid doesn't have to only begin on the first day of school. You can begin to make a difference by being different on any day of the school year. Even today.

66

Before Raising Academic Expectations for Struggling Students, They Must First Experience Evidence of Academic Achievement

I love when children participate in sports, especially little league baseball and softball. Not the type of leagues where teams don't keep score, everyone is celebrated as a winner, and all "winners" receive a shiny trophy at the end of the season just for showing up. Rather, I'm talking about leagues where boys and girls are coached to develop teamwork, skill, work ethic and yes – as traumatizing as it may sound – scores are kept and sometimes kids win, and other times kids lose.

I particularly love watching the kids take their turns batting during the games. I study their body language when they're in the on-deck circle knowing they're up next. As the player walks from the on-deck circle to the batter's box, I can pretty much predict what's going to happen – whether a kid is going to strikeout or get a hit.

Some kids step-up to the plate with such assuredness. The way they move, the way they breathe, the way they gesture – they're filled with absolute confidence. It's the kind of confidence that stems from kids having a wealth of successful experiences hitting the ball. In their minds, those kids have a stockpile of positive batting experiences upon which they can draw. Even as they continue playing year after year, facing more difficult pitching, they continue to progress right along as successful hitters.

For other kids, however, the opposite is true. As they walk to the batter's box, it's equally obvious what's going to happen. The way they move, the way they breathe, the way they gesture – they're filled with a sense a defeat even before the first pitch is thrown to them. It's clear that they're going to strikeout. And, as those kids continue playing year after year, facing more difficult pitching, they will struggle even worse right up until the point when they decide to give up. No one can handle feeling like a failure year after year. It's easier to just quit.

The same is true for our kids in our classrooms. For those kids with a history of academic success, they will continue to thrive as they're able to draw upon their stockpile of previous successful experiences as the academic demands and expectations increase. However, those students who struggle in the classroom year after year are going to continue to struggle and feel defeated as the academic demands and expectations increase. And, just like in baseball, they will struggle even worse right up until the point when they decide to give up. Remember, no one can handle feeling like a failure year after year. It's easier to just quit.

The first step to increasing rigor and raising expectations must be to create positive academic experiences for those kids who struggle, feel defeated, and have quit. As their teacher, it's critical that you create scenarios where they can experience the thrill of success and the emotions created by achievement. Am I talking about a contrived moment where we can hand them a shiny participation trophy just for showing up? Absolutely not. I'm talking about creating authentic opportunities for small successes that have a positive, emotional impact. The more real wins, no matter how small, a kid can feel ownership of, the more they'll want to step up to bat in their own education.

67

Student Success Is Not about Curriculum, School Leadership, or Funding; It's about YOU

I live in Houston, Texas, the epicenter of the oil and gas industry. A few years ago, I received a call from one of the largest oil and gas companies in the world. I was asked if I would meet with them at their corporate offices about a project they were working on for giving back to the communities where they were currently drilling. I was told, "We are committed to playing a role in supporting schools by making a difference in the lives of teachers and students."

You should know that when an O&G company rolls into a small, rural community to drill for oil, life dramatically changes for the people who have lived in that town for generations. Within a matter of weeks, the once quiet town becomes overrun with trucks and machinery and the population more than doubles with temporary workers. As a result, the infrastructure is destroyed, roads are decimated, the cost of living and the crime rate sky-rocket, and schools are pushed beyond the breaking point as the student population grows exponentially.

The representative of the O&G company informed me that the plan was to invest in a supplemental STEAM curriculum to provide to the local school district. They thought this would surely make up for the devastation and hardship brought to the families of the town.

As I stepped into the beautifully decorated conference room, the committee members were already circled around the large, imported, marble table. Two STEAM curriculums were meticulously organized and laid out in separate piles. The committee chairperson spoke up and got right to the point, "We're going to make a significant investment in one of these curriculums. Which one is best? Which one should we go with?"

I couldn't help myself. I pointed to the first curriculum and said, "This one is a pile of garbage. It's absolutely terrible." They all stared at me in silence, apparently shocked by my abruptness. After I let that sink in for a few seconds, I added, "That is, this curriculum is terrible if the teacher is terrible." Then, without hesitation, I pointed at the second pile. "That one sucks, too. If the teacher sucks." And, since I didn't want to be totally discouraging, I also offered, "However, if you put either of those programs in the hands of an awesome, world class teacher, they will be equally awesome and world class programs." I added, "If you want to know the effectiveness of a curriculum, show me the teacher not the curriculum."

Please understand, I know that not all curriculum is created equal and that they all have their strengths and weaknesses. But my point is you just can't throw money at buying new programs and curriculum thinking that's going to somehow magically increase student achievement. Weak teachers will continue to struggle no matter the curriculum. Strong teachers will continue to thrive no matter the curriculum.

Does curriculum, resources, funding, administration, and 100 other things play a role in successfully educating children? Yes, of course. But, what's always been true and will forever remain true is this: The single most important determining factor in the education of students will forever be YOU – their teacher.

There is no other ingredient in the recipe of student success that is more important than you.

By the way, if you're wondering which curriculum they picked, they didn't. Just a few weeks after our meeting there was a downturn in the oil and gas market and they immediately disbanded the committee, terminated the project, and did absolutely nothing to help the local schools. Apparently, they weren't all that "committed to playing a role in supporting schools by making a difference in the lives of teachers and students." Imagine that.

You and I both know that there's only one person our children can count on to believe in them, teach them, and love them. And, that person is you.

68

You Are the Architect and Carpenter of Classroom Culture; Envision, Design, and Build the Family Your Students Deserve

I grew up in a typical, quiet, middle class neighborhood. Everything about it was typical, quiet, and middle class – the people, the stores, the schools, the landscaping, and especially the houses. All the houses were close to identical with only a few variations here and there. In fact, when I rode my bicycle around the neighborhood I would sometimes get confused as to where I was because all the streets looked the same.

But when I went to visit friends in the neighborhood, and stepped inside their homes, I found that what was happening inside houses were far from identical. The differences were shocking. I'm not talking about the interior décor. I'm referring to what was happening in the home. Inside, every house had its own unique feel and culture. Mark's home was always loud with people yelling back-and-forth at one another. At Roger's house, you had better be prepared to be hugged – by everyone. Stanton's home felt stoic with people sitting around, reading in silence. I never saw anyone in Vincent's house. Everyone stayed in their individual rooms with the door closed. Walter's house had rules, lots and lots of rules. At my house, you were greeted with laughter and snacks. Pringles, Bugles, Fritos, pretzels, crackers – if it crunched, we had it and we served it.

When I work with teachers I often hear, "Well, you're giving us all these great ideas, but they would never work in my school. We just don't have that kind of school culture." Or, they tell me, "That wouldn't fly where I teach, we just don't have those kinds of kids."

Does the culture of a school affect what's happening inside an individual classroom? For some teachers, absolutely. Their classrooms are an exact representation of what's happening on campus. However, other teachers have the ability to create a classroom culture that is individually distinctive to their personality, their teaching style, and their classroom family.

I think you would agree with me that you can walk down the hall of the most quiet, controlled, reserved school and find a classroom that is completely out of control with kids screaming and jumping from desk to desk. And, the opposite is also true. You can find the most loving, organized, productive classroom in a school where kids are completely out of control, running wild in the hallways.

Classrooms in a school are no different than homes in a neighborhood. Kids will adopt the culture that is consistently and solidly established in a family, whether that family be inside of a home or inside of a classroom. At Mark's house we were loud. At Roger's house we hugged. At Stanton's we didn't say a word. At Vincent's house we hung out in his room. At Walter's house we followed lots and lots of rules. And, at my house we laughed and snacked.

As a teacher, it's solely up to you to provide a classroom for your students that serves as a home and a family. You are the architect and carpenter of culture in your classroom. It's your job to envision it, design it, and build it. Then, once established, consistently reinforced, and solidly held in place, your kids will accept it, embrace it, and live it. And, as your students continue to move through life, they will exhibit the love and respect of your classroom which served as the home and family in which they were raised.

69

Students Sometimes Ask Us Their Most Important Questions with Behaviors, Rather than Words

There is no soft or sweet way to say it. On some days, being a teacher can feel like Dante's Inferno. And, there's no day of the school year more difficult than when the 13th day of the month falls on a Friday during a full moon. The triple whammy. The only people who don't believe that human beings go a little nuts during a full-moon, especially on a Friday the 13th, are those who don't work in schools, law enforcement, or emergency rooms.

This particular full-moon Friday the 13th was like no other. Simply put, the kids were absolutely insane. In my classroom, the day began with a focus on project-based learning with high-level differentiated instruction. Within minutes, I transitioned my focus to yelling. Lots of yelling. Then, more yelling. And then, louder yelling.

That night at home, as I sat on the couch considering other career options, my daughter toddled over and climbed up next to me with her favorite book, "I Love You Stinky Face" written by Lisa McCourt and illustrated by Cyd Moore.

If you're not familiar with this book, it's about a boy who asks his mom if she would continue to love him even if he was a stinky skunk, or a swamp creature, or a bug eating green alien from Mars. Throughout the book, his mom consistently assures him that she will love him forever, no matter what.

At this point in my life, I've read "I Love You Stinky Face" to my daughter a few hundred times. But, I never thought about it like I did on that evening. It occurred to me that the question, "Will you love me forever, no matter what?" is something each and every one of our students are asking us. However, they don't typically use their words. They usually ask us with their behaviors.

As I continued to read, I thought back to my classroom earlier in the day. There were lots of stinky skunks, swamp creatures, and bug eating green alien from Mars running wild with their behaviors clearly asking if I would love them forever, no matter what. I realized that as I was drowning in the emotions of anger and frustration that day, I only responded with yelling. In fact, that's all I could remember about the day – me yelling. Now with my daughter falling asleep in my lap, I wondered if my students were also falling asleep, thinking about their days, only able to remember me yelling.

On Monday morning, we began with a classroom family meeting. We discussed what happened on Friday. We talked. We shared. We took responsibility. Then, together, we read "I Love You Stinky Face." My students took turns reading the part of the boy, while I read the part of the mom. A student read aloud, "But, Mama, but, Mama, what if I were a swamp creature with slimy, smelly seaweed hanging from my body?" In my best Mama voice, I replied, "Then I would live by the swamp and take care of you always. I'd tell you, 'I love you my slimy swamp monster!'" Another student continued, "But Mama, but Mama, what if I were a green alien from Mars and I ate bugs instead of peanut butter?" I replied, "Then I would fill your lunch box with spiders and ants and the tastiest bugs you ever had! And I'd pack a note with all the bugs that said, 'I love you little greenie. Bon Appétit!'"

As we finished the book, there was lots of laughter, tears, and apologies shared by all. Yes, including me. Just before we adjourned our family meeting to begin class, I announced, "Hey Fam, look up at me. Look into my eyes as I tell you this. You are all my Stinky Faces and I will love you forever, no matter what."

70

Maslow before Bloom

One of the most common themes in education is Maslow before Bloom and the point of it is that students have certain physical needs that need to be met before their learning needs can be met. However, I believe that this is true of teachers too.

Every year teachers have more added to their plates without anything taken off their plates. The worst part is when the explanations are things like, "it's for the kids," "it's not about you; it's about the kids," or "it's the way we have always done it." But the reality is that students learn in an environment created by you, and if you don't feel supported, encouraged, and appreciated, then it's hard to create a dynamic learning environment, especially on a consistent basis. So, whether or not you get all the support you need from your administration, please make sure you are taking care of yourself and your teammates. We have heard the old adage that you can't pour from an empty cup and it is an accurate reflection of teaching. It is hard to inspire others when you feel constantly run down yourself.

So, don't feel like you are being selfish when you take care of yourself, but realize if you aren't at your best, then you can't give your best. Some ideas for taking care of yourself during the school day include; getting your class up and moving, doing some deep breathing or stretches with your class or during a break, and going outside and getting fresh air, even if you have to use class time.

Finally, leave school at school as often as you can. The work will be there waiting for you the next day. If you don't separate work and home, then the lines will blur and you may never recover. Spend time with family and friends, or simply take an hour for yourself in a bubble bath. Whatever it takes for you to refuel and refill your cup!

71

Follow Your Path

Now this is a great piece of advice whether you are focusing on your career or in your personal life. As a teacher, we often feel pressure to be more like the awesome teacher down the hall or the expert who just provided professional development. But the reality is you are an amazing teacher in your own right or you at least have the potential within you to be. The key is to use your talents and follow your heart as you hone your skills as a teacher. The same can be said in your personal life, where people have certain expectations of you or you feel like you have expectations that you have placed on yourself.

I felt this way early in life, but in my twenties, my father shared a piece of advice that I never forgot and it's the premise of the above quote. It was actually one of the last pieces of advice he gave me, right before he passed away much too soon in life. He said, "Son, follow your own path. Don't worry what others say or do or even what you think is expected, but follow your path." My father may not have known just how impactful that piece of advice was to me, then again, he may have known it was exactly the words that I needed to hear. Either way, I am so thankful that I listened.

As a teacher, administrator, professor, author, and speaker, I have always followed my own path. I felt pressured by others at times to take a certain position or not to take a certain risk, but I stayed true to my path. So, don't feel like you have to live up to others expectations, or do things like someone else. You have to follow your path. As I look back on my life, I have to say this was probably one of the most important pieces of advice I ever received and I am glad that I listened and followed my father's advice. I think you will be glad you did too!

72

Be Fully Present!

Have you ever attended a meeting and said present when they called your name, but then for most of the meeting, you weren't really present or at least you weren't fully present? Or have you asked for a meeting with someone, like your administrator, and they spent most of their time checking their phone, or preoccupied with something else?

There is a difference between present and being fully present. This is not just true in school but in our everyday life as well. For instance, we always like to talk about being in the moment, but the reality is that that most people are only paying full attention in the present moment, 50% of the time. That means we basically miss out on half our life, with our attention somewhere other than in the moment.

It is important to be in the moment; to be fully present with your students. You never know what you may be missing if you are just going through the motions or your mind is elsewhere. Just as you want your administrator's full attention, focus on giving your students that same kind of attention. It may change how they interact and engage in the classroom.

Finally, learn to be focused on the moment whether you are at school or home. It can be easy to be on autopilot with your day-to-day schedule, but it is important to spice it up a bit each day so that you are able to actually enjoy the present. We are creatures of habit and often when we are in the "fray of the day" we turn on autopilot and in those instances we don't fully engage. Giving your full attention means you value the people or the activities in which you are engaged. So, don't just seize the moment, but seize the fullness of it.

73

Become More Goal Driven

I know we all have been told that dreams aren't attainable until we write them down, and then they become goals which are attainable. And we have been told to have short term goals and long terms and be focused on them. But the reality is we often don't take the time to set goals and then revisit them to measure our achievement. I have taught leadership classes for the past few years and the one thing I encourage all students to do is become experts at setting and achieving goals.

I have been fortunate to interview some of the top leaders from every industry (business, military, sports, education, entertainment) over the past 10 years and they had a few characteristics in common. Now when very successful people share common traits, it makes you pay attention to those traits. One of them was that they all set goals. Daily, weekly, monthly, yearly, and long term goals. They used these goals to measure their progress. Imagine having a weight loss goal, or a fitness goal, but you never stop to measure your success. Otherwise, how do you know if you are succeeding or not? How do you know if you are making progress?

I remember sitting down several years ago and writing out my long-term goals. I wanted to get my doctoral degree because I thought it would give me validity for my one major goal which was to write books. As a former jock and the first one in my family to graduate college both goals may have seemed out of reach, but I believed in myself and I set goals to plan out my success. Well, I am a doctor and 10 books later, I am still writing. Never give up on your dreams, but just make sure you have a roadmap of goals to help you achieve them!

74

Everything in Life Boils Down to Relationships

While we all may dream of days, or maybe even weeks, where we could just be alone, the reality is that every aspect of our lives is based upon relationships. Whether it is with a spouse, family, friends, colleagues, or even students, everything is based upon relationships.

Since so much of our existence is based upon these relationships it is important to make sure we have healthy relationships. I like to joke that I had a former principal who said we were going to be like family. But what he didn't tell us was that it was a dysfunctional family! Now you may have experienced a situation like this or maybe you are currently in this type of situation. If so, just remember you can help make these relationships more positive.

Most relationships are formed based upon a level of respect or love and every healthy relationship needs trust. So, whether it is your students, colleagues, or your administrators, make sure you create a relationship based upon respect and trust. And relationships are important in the school setting because you spend over 1,000 hours a year with your students and that doesn't count all the hours with your colleagues and teammates. If you think about it, during the school year you may spend as much of your waking hours at school as at home. So, don't underestimate the importance of building those relationships. But at the same time, as I am known to say, make sure those that are important to you also get the best of you and not just what is left of you. So, make sure you are nurturing those personal relationships with family and friends as well.

75

The Worry Tree

When it comes to our personal lives, I think there is a balance we have to strike with students. For instance, it is important for them to see we are human and that we have real world problems. But, have you ever met teachers who bring all their baggage to the classroom every day? I try to help these teachers realize that many of their students have their own issues that they are dealing with and they are looking for an adult who is supportive and positive rather than down and out themselves. Remember, it's ok, to have a bad day, but try not to have them often or let them affect the classroom. Leadership is all about influence and you as the leader of the classroom have influence on the climate of the class.

There is an old tale of a carpenter who had a worry tree outside of his home where he would figuratively place his worries of the day before he entered into his home to be with his family. He said he might have troubles at work, but that doesn't mean his family needed to worry about them to, so he left them outside until morning. So, try as much as possible to leave your worries at the door when you walk into the classroom each morning and focus on the day with your kids. In fact, put a hanger there to symbolically leave them as you walk into class. Then when you get home, hang your professional worries outside before you walk in the door. This way you don't bring your work problems home for your family or friends to worry about.

As the story goes, the carpenter said the next morning when he picked up the worries, they were much lighter than when he left them. Try this, it might just lighten your worries as well!

76

Take the Time to Tell Your Students What You Needed to Hear When You Were Their Age

I attend a lot of professional development sessions. I'm constantly on the hunt for something new and creative that I can share with educators as I travel across the country speaking at schools and conferences. We all know that the best educators are the best thieves. That is, they find something that works; they steal it; they customize it to fit their personalities and teaching styles; then, they use it in their classrooms. Providing professional development to teachers works the same way. When I attend conferences, my goal is to find at least one nugget of information I can steal, make it better, and share it with you.

Recently, I attended a small PD session and I was on the hunt for that nugget. It's kind of like panning for gold. On that day, it seemed like I stood in the stream of information for six hours and was yet to find that gold nugget. As the session was coming to a close, the presenter said, "Before we leave, we're going to do an activity called 'The Calling of the Angels.'" I immediately looked for the door and strategized how I could get out before I had to endure the "angel calling." But, because there was no easy escape, I decided to just tough it out for the last few minutes.

The presenter asked half of us to form a circle with our chairs and sit down facing the center of the circle. The remaining half were asked to stand behind someone who was sitting.

Our presenter began her introduction to the activity: "I would like everyone to close their eyes." At this point, it was all

I could do to not disengage from the moment as I usually don't enjoy these types of activities. But, I thought to myself, "I'll just go along and commit to this and I'll just see where it goes." Our presenter continued,

> Keeping your eyes closed, I want you to go back in time to when you were in school. Go back to a time when you were struggling and really needed someone to care for you. It might be when you were in elementary school, or middle school, or maybe high school. Think about a specific challenging event or situation that was happening in your life on a particular day. I would like you to remember those painful emotions and re-experience what that felt like.

Our presenter continued with her instructions and I'll be the first to admit: She was amazing. I kept my eyes closed and didn't peek, but with the amount of sniffling I could hear in the room I knew that everyone was re-experiencing a painful moment from their childhood.

After she got everyone to a place where they were reliving their childhood moment she asked, "What did you need to hear on that day? Was there an adult in your life whose support you needed? What did you need from them? What do you wish they said?" She then gave us our final instructions.

> Those of you standing, I would like you to place your hands on the shoulders of the person sitting before you, lean down and whisper to that person whatever it was that you needed to hear on that day as a child. Then, you'll move to the next person sitting in the circle, and then the next. Those of you sitting, keep your eyes closed and just simply listen. Once we make a full rotation around the circle, we'll switch places.

She then dimmed the lights and played Sara McLachlan's "In the Arms of an Angel." That's when it got really emotional.

Person after person came up behind me and whispered into my ear exactly what they needed to hear on that painful day when they were a child.

It's no coincidence that what they needed to hear, was exactly what I needed to hear. But, what was fascinating was that the same phrases were repeated over and over. They were all some form of . . .

I accept you. I appreciate you. I believe in you. I am proud of you. I love you. The experience was incredibly moving and one that I will never forget.

As I drove home from the conference that evening, I thought a lot about those five short sentences, and I thought a lot about my students. It occurred to me that with so many kids in my classes there was a good chance that at least one kid in class needed to hear one of those phrases on any given day.

We'll never really know all the details of what's happening in the lives of our student's outside of our classrooms. But, I do know this: Right now, there are kids in our classrooms who are facing challenges that are incredibly difficult and excruciatingly painful. And, sometimes just a few words can simplify that difficulty and alleviate that pain. Please, take every opportunity to speak to the heart and soul of your kids and let them know, "I accept you. I appreciate you. I believe in you. I am proud of you. I love you."

77

Create a Classroom That Is a Buzzing, Exciting, and Electrifying "Workshop" for Learning

I recently heard a lot about a small high school in rural East Texas with an incredible Career and Technology Education program. I'm passionate about providing kids with an education that fits their interests and their natural talents and abilities. So, I made the 10-hour drive just to see this program for myself.

Whoever told me that this CTE program at this country school was incredible was not being completely truthful. It was beyond incredible. It was astoundingly awesome.

I arrived at the school at 7am so I could chat with the principal for a bit before school started at 8am. She immediately asked me if I wanted to see their CTE facilities. I suggested we should wait an hour until the kids arrived. She laughed and told me, "I'm here at 5am every morning and I have a line of kids waiting for me to unlock the doors to the workshop."

The workshop – the CTE facility – is a large warehouse structure that sits behind the school, next to the football field. When I walked in it was busy, loud, and was buzzing with energy! It sounded, looked, and felt like education should – active and exciting. There were kids welding. There were kids machining parts on a lathe. Kids were laser cutting sheet metal. Small groups were gathered around small engines. Larger groups were gathered around larger engines. Kids were cutting, sanding, and staining cabinetry. There was so much I loved about what I saw on that day. From the level of passion for learning demonstrated by the kids to how well everyone – without exception – followed the systems and procedures put in place to create a safe, respectful, and productive environment. It was exhilarating to watch!

It took a while, but once I got used to the sounds, energy, and controlled chaos of the facility I was finally able to notice the teachers. Typically, when I enter a classroom the first thing I notice and pay attention to is the teacher. They're usually at the front of the classroom leading the lesson. This classroom was very different. There were four teachers spaced throughout the workshop. All four were intensely focused on watching the kids work. They were all constantly scanning the area, not just observing, but more like they were analyzing the activity. I noticed a group of kids working on an old John Deere tractor when they all looked over their shoulders toward their teacher who made an immediate beeline to their work area. Because of the volume, I couldn't hear the interaction but what I saw was a student pointing at the engine, explaining, while the teacher listened and nodded. I watched their teacher motion for another student across the workshop. The student came over to the tractor and took over for the teacher who went back to his spot to continue watching, observing, and analyzing.

Later that day I had lunch with the CTE teachers who explained it all in very simple terms for me.

> We watch those kids like hawks not just because we don't want anyone getting hurt, but also because we can't hear with all that loud machinery. So, if a group has a question, all they have to do is look at an instructor and we'll immediately head that way.

I asked, "Why not have students raise their hand like in a typical academic class?" He set me straight. "Sir, remember we can't hear well in there. So, raising your hand means you have an emergency. If you have a question, just look our way."

I then asked if he would tell me about the kid who came over to help with the tractor. He told me,

> Those boys and girls were working on the pistons on that old John Deere and they were confused. Jonathan,

that kid I called for, is basically the shop expert on tractor engines. So, I called him over. The way we set up our shop is to have kids learning from other kids as much as possible. That way, our expert students have a chance to deepen their expertise by teaching what they know; our kids get to learn from their peers; it creates a desire for younger students to become experts; and, it allows me to get back to watching for other kids who might need help.

On my drive home the next day I couldn't help but think about how the inherent challenges of that CTE "classroom" – the volume, the amount of students, the chaos, multiple work stations, the potential for injury – all helped to create such an outstanding learning environment. But I think the real takeaway from my visit was that those inherent challenges are not required to create that style of classroom culture. I know that in any class-room, in any school, and in any content area, we can create an academic "workshop" that is alive and buzzing with learning; overflowing with passionate learners; a place where expertise is celebrated; and, where teachers facilitate learning rather than impose learning.

78

Partner with an Educator You Love to Dig Down and Discover the Deepest Reason WHY You Teach, Then, Share It with Your Students

Why do you teach? That's a question that I regularly ask teachers. It's not a simple question with a simple answer, that's for sure. And, it's certainly not a topic that teachers are used to discussing. I have always found that fact interesting. Think about it: Teaching is the most important, most honorable profession on the planet. It's filled with professionals who are more creative, resourceful, educated, and degreed than any other profession. Educators could easily transition to any other professional sector and make more money with less stress. Yet, we never engage in deep and meaningful conversations about WHY we choose to come back year after year to work with kids and do the job that means so much to us.

I think we don't talk about WHY we teach on a deep level because it's a hard conversation requiring a lot of emotional effort. That is, because teaching is such an emotionally complex and deeply challenging profession, it takes a lot of work and energy to dig down, through all the emotion, to search for and find the most fundamental answer to such a big question.

So, I ask you: Why do you teach? A teacher's initial answer to that question is usually something like, "Because I love it." I'll admit that initial answer does sound like a deep and meaningful reason. However, lots of experience with this conversation has taught me that answer is actually just the tip of the iceberg of deeper reasons that lie beneath the surface. "Because I love it" may sound deep, but it's actually the most superficial reason of all. There's always more to the answer than that.

Whenever I hear that initial answer, I'll always affirm the answer and then ask WHY again. "I can tell you absolutely do love it. But, what if you dig a little deeper? Tell me, WHY do you love it?" And, that's when the work begins. Since most educators have never really thought about it deeper than that initial, superficial reason, it definitely takes some time and effort to get to the bottom of it all – the real reason. So, I'll continue affirming and asking WHY and they will continue answering. As soon as they answer with a reason that's a little bit deeper, I'll affirm and follow with, "Dig even deeper. WHY is that?"

Eventually, there will be a moment when a teacher finally just stares at me and she'll say, "I don't know, I guess that's just what it is. That's it." And, I'll know we're there. It's obvious when we've arrived at the deepest, most fundamental reason of all when there is no next answer to the WHY question.

Here's my challenge to you. Partner with another teacher – one who you love and connect with – and go through the process of digging into your WHY. Ask each other, "Why do you teach?" Start with intentionally replying to the question with the most easy, superficial reasons you could possibly come up with. Then, take turns asking each other, "Why is that?" Then, work together to find, identify, and articulate the next deepest reason. Once you identify and discuss those reasons, follow it again with, "Why is that?" Together, continue holding each other accountable and keep digging down until you both arrive at your individual, deepest, most fundamental reason of all. Then, and most importantly, boldly and clearly share that WHY with those students you love and serve each and every day.

79

There's No Other Profession on the Planet Where You Can Impact the Trajectory of a Generation

As teachers, we spend a lot of time talking about changing the lives of our kids. And we should. That's what this job is all about – using the content of our classrooms to have a lifelong impact on the lives of our students. Not just impacting what they know, but more importantly, who they're becoming.

However, I think sometimes we get so caught up on having a dramatic, positive affect on the people inside of our classrooms, we forget to recognize the impact we're having on the people outside of our classrooms.

Early in my teaching career I read an article written by a sociologist whose research suggested that every person living in a modern, first-world society will have an impact on 10,000 other lives over the course of their lifetime. How amazing is that? On average, from the day of their first breath to the day of their last breath, each person will have a direct impact on 10,000 other people.

Now, take a moment and apply that research to your classroom.

Remember, when we're focused on changing the life of a kid, we're not just talking about that one, individual child. We're also talking about the 10,000 lives that kid will go on to impact. How many kids do you have in your class? Let's say it's 23. Again, is teaching all about the positive difference you can make with those 23 kids in your classroom? Of course, it is. But, it's also about the 230,000 people those students will go onto impact. If you want to see just how monumental of an impact a single teacher can have, consider those elementary teachers who have hundreds of students rotating through their specific content areas, such as an art teacher. Or, what about those teachers in intermediate school, middle school, and high school who have dozens of kids in five, six, or seven periods per day. The work they do each year will have an impact on millions.

Take a moment to calculate the "Total World Impact" you've had so far in your career. Use the formula:

(Number of years teaching) x (Average number of students per year) x 10,000 = Total World Impact

If you're like most people, after you plug the numbers into the formula and then hit = on your calculator and see that giant number, you're going to assume you did the math incorrectly. You'll think, "Surely that can't be correct. That number is too big." Well, it is correct. The impact is that big.

So, please remember, as you're working to instill those qualities like love, acceptance, courage, and forgiveness in your kids. You're also instilling those same qualities in millions upon millions of people your kids will go onto impact.

The only place on the planet where you can impact, not just the lives of individual kids, but also millions of lives across multiple generations of a society is in your classroom. Thank you for accepting such a tremendous responsibility.

80

Passion and Purpose Are Two Required Ingredients in the Recipe of a Great Teacher

It was the middle of March when I received a call from a principal friend of mine. I had been to her intermediate school to work with her staff many times in the past, but not in the last couple of years. She said,

> I have a number of first-year teachers on my staff this year. There are three of them that I just can't figure out how to help. Their kids are struggling academically, and they just don't seem to fit in with our campus culture. I've sent them to every PD I could find, set them up with mentors, gave them books to read, worked on classroom procedures, but nothing seems to help. Would you please come spend the day on campus, observe them, and tell me what you think we can do to help them?

"Yes! Of course," I said. "I'll be there tomorrow." I showed up early to campus because I love to watch how they greet their kids in the morning. It's exciting, to say the least. Every adult on campus participates as they all gather where the kids get dropped off in the morning to welcome the kids to school. As I'm watching the hundreds of high-fives and hugs and cheers for kids arriving at school, I noticed three young teachers off to the side, huddled-up together, chatting as they looked at their phones. I immediately thought to myself, "I bet those are the three I'm here to see."

I was right. The plan was that I would spend a couple hours in each of the three teachers' classrooms, and then the principal and I would get back together in the afternoon to debrief.

I showed up in the first classroom at 8:00am. I sat down in the back corner as kids were walking around just doing their own thing while their teacher sat at her desk, still scrolling on her phone. The morning announcements began with the pledge of allegiance. Nothing changed – kids still not paying attention, their teacher still sitting at her desk, still on her phone. I noticed the date on the board was over a week old. I'm assuming that was also true for the "Objective and Focus" that was printed beneath the date. After about five minutes I had seen enough. I knew exactly what the issue was. I went to the second classroom.

As I walked in, the young teacher in front of the class was reading from his social studies teacher's edition textbook. The room was quiet, but, again, kids were just doing their own thing. I saw headphones in ears, a couple were playing games on their phones, and lots of kids were just staring out the window. Then I saw one girl crying. I saw another boy who was obviously sick – extremely sick. I'm a parent so I know what fever looks like. Their teacher didn't notice either kid. I immediately sent the principal a text to send her counselor to come get the two kids. At this point, I had seen enough. I knew exactly what the issue was, and I left.

As I entered the third classroom the lights were off, a video was playing, most of the kids were sleeping, and I could smell the distinct odor of fingernail polish. I looked up and there was their teacher at her desk whispering and giggling on her phone while painting her nails. I didn't sit down. I just left and headed for the principal's office. I had seen enough. I knew exactly what the issue was.

I walked through the front office and I saw the little sick boy in the nurse's office, and I saw the counselor hugging the little girl as she continued to cry. As I stepped into the principal's office she said, "It's not even 8:30am, and you're back already? Tell me what you think." I didn't tell her what I thought. I told her what I knew.

Here's the issue. They're just not teachers. It's as simple as that. Based on what I saw – and I saw more than enough to know for sure – there's no amount of support or training or mentoring that can help them become who they're not. I'm not saying they're bad people. I'm sure they're wonderful people. They're just not teachers.

She was nodding in agreement, so I continued.

Even if you're a first-year teacher with no experience, but you're passionate about teaching and your purpose is to make a difference in the lives of kids, that alone is going to make you an acceptable educator. From there, we can provide the information, support, and guidance you need to become good. Then, with enough experience, you can become great. These three just don't have the fundamental, main ingredients that are required to be acceptable, let alone good. Teaching is not their passion and it's not their purpose.

I looked her in her eyes as I finished,

I think your job, as the campus leader, is to serve your school and your kids by empowering those three young teachers with the confidence and self-awareness needed to realize this career just isn't for them. Because, in their hearts, they already know it to be true.

People know just how much I love amazing teachers – those incredible people whose passion and purpose it is to show up every day to create a classroom family where lifelong relationships are built; kids are loved relentlessly; and lives are changed. But what people don't realize is that I equally love those people who become teachers only to realize it's just not for them, it's not who they are, and they move on to find another way to make a difference in the lives of others outside of the classroom. It's what's best for them. It's what's best for our schools. And, most importantly, it's what's best for our kids.

81

Never Give Up!

We know teaching is a tough career because nearly half of teachers leave the profession within the first five years. But if you are committed to educating our youth, don't give up. There is an old saying that you should never give up on something you think about often. I think that is true, especially of teachers. We think about kids, even when we aren't with them. Teachers are great at never giving up on their students, but how committed are you to yourself? Whether it is honing your craft as a teacher or possibly doing more with your teaching skills, never give up!

You may be going through a tough year professionally or even personally and you may just want to give up, but hang in there. While I am not a big fan of Harry Potter, I am a fan of the perseverance that J. K. Rowling showed when she was writing it. She was recently divorced, living on government assistance, trying to take care of a baby as a single mom, and she had to write the manuscript on a typewriter because she didn't have a computer. When she completed it she was then rejected 12 times by publishers before a small publishing house decided to take a chance on an unknown writer. Where would she be now if she just felt like giving up before the thirteenth publisher?

Coach John Wooden, who I have mentioned as the greatest basketball coach of all time, and who won 12 national championships, also struggled. In fact, he coached for 18 years before he got the first championship. What if he had quit after the seventeenth season?

So, believe in yourself. Believe that this too shall pass, and that you can keep going. And what better inspiration for your students, who you never give up on, than to see that you never give up on yourself?

82

Don't Let Others Steal Your Joy!

I have often said that the problem with happiness is that too many people are looking for it when they should be creating it. The same is true of joy in that it is all around us if we take a moment and realize it. Most people never find a job that is as fulfilling and rewarding as teaching. Yes, it is the toughest job in the world, but it is also a job that brings great joy. I can remember waking up my first year of teaching, and although I was often tired, I felt such a joy to be doing something I truly loved.

So don't lose that joy of teaching and being in the noblest of professions. I admit that at times it can be easy to feel defeated, joyless, and unsatisfied, but even if you aren't in the ideal school setting or supported as much as you like, just focus on the things in your life that are great. I have walked into schools where it seems the energy is zapped out of me as I enter the door, and I've asked myself who stole their joy? Who or what is keeping this staff from enjoying their job? Then I've walked into schools where the energy is electric! Where everyone has a smile and is engaging. Students pick up on the vibes of the staff and the energy you give off affects your classroom.

I used to tell my graduate students that the best way to keep your joy is not to let others get you down. Not to listen to people who criticize or try to keep you down. This doesn't mean that you shouldn't be willing to accept feedback or critique, but I am talking more about the constant critics. I have a rule that I don't listen to the feedback of people who don't value me or who I don't value. If I don't value someone's praise then I am certainly not listening to their critiques. Never give others that much control over your life. Remember that when you walk into the classroom, you have the opportunity to positively affect the lives of your students and that alone should be enough to bring you joy!

83

Finding Your Voice

Did you know that teachers, more than workers in any other profession, feel like their voice is not heard and they are not valued? I know this can be frustrating, especially since you are a well-educated and trained professional with many great ideas. But rather than continue to be frustrated in silence, look for ways to find and share your voice in meaningful ways.

Voice is creating an overall expression of who you are ... to yourself, to your community, and to the world. Your voice will allow you to communicate your needs and wants while contributing your talents and capabilities. Your expression is the culmination of finding, creating, and using your voice to make a difference for yourself and your life. Discovering your values, creating outcomes, sharing your influence, developing courage, and conveying your overall expression are all ingredients for finding and using your voice as a leader.

So, when it comes to your student or education issues in general, don't be afraid to speak up, especially on topics that you are passionate about. As an administrator, I would encourage teachers to speak up on topics of passion to them, because I knew that if they saw problems, then they should be addressed, and if they were passionate, then I know they would seek out the best solutions for those issues.

Don't let fear or defeating self-talk like "I am just a teacher" keep you from finding your voice. Also, don't let others drown out your voice with negativity, especially your inner voice. In fact, when you have the courage to speak up, you may inspire others to find their voices as well. You need and deserve to be heard, you are the expert in the classroom after all!

84

Becoming Emotionally Connected

I think most every teacher is what we call a people person, which means you probably have a higher level of EQ, or emotional intelligence. A high degree of emotional intelligence has many benefits. For example, increased self-awareness helps you respond better to the day-to-day situations you face personally and professionally. Emotional intelligence will help you address certain stressful situations in which your actions can impact students' learning and well-being. Also, it helps you deal with the new challenges that come with problematic groups of students, crowded classrooms, or a lack of student motivation.

I remember several years ago that I had a couple of students who were shy, didn't seem to have many friends, and often kept to themselves. I planned a videogame party for my students because I knew that those shy students enjoyed a game called *Halo* and I also knew from talking to them that they were pretty good at the game. Well by the end of the evening, all the other boys wanted them on their teams to play. The following Monday in my classes, the boys were engaged in class and with their newfound friends. I had one father actually stop by school and thank me because he said it was all his son talked about. I did those events for several years and the results were always amazing.

Now you don't have to take on a task of that level to build an emotional connectedness with your students. But getting a sense of what is going on in their lives and remembering what it was like to be their age certainly can help you empathize with them and hopefully make the class or school year a little better.

85

You Are a Leader

One word I have come to loathe over the past 25 years is "teacher-leader." You aren't teacher-leaders but you are a leader. There is no need for a hyphen! In fact, I have said many times, even in tweets, that some of the best leaders in the school are in the classroom, not in the front office or central office. Great teachers possess characteristics of leadership – integrity, commitment, effective communication, passion, expertise, and, maybe most importantly, a servant's heart.

The most effective leadership type is servant leadership and teachers possess many, if not all, of the characteristics of this style. Servant leaders are other focused, inspirational, encouraging, supportive, affirmational, and seek to help improve the lives of those they lead. Doesn't this sound like you? Yes! In fact, it sounds like most of the teachers I know, and I know a lot of teachers!

If you feel like you struggle as a leader in the classroom just remember that there are processes you can put into place to help you be more effective. Building authentic relationships with students is the foundation, but also make sure to establish clear routines and high expectations for your students. These not only show your leadership ability but make running the classroom so much easier. So, be prepared to lead every day in the classroom, and as you build your leadership confidence, seek other leadership opportunities as well, whether in the school or outside the school. You are not just a teacher, you are also a leader!

86

Use the Content of Your Classroom to Impact the Character of Your Kids

For the last decade, I've been traveling from coast-to-coast speaking to educators at schools and conferences. People always ask me, "Do you ever get sick of being on the road?" I definitely get tired of airports and rental cars and small-town motels, but the payoff definitely makes up for it. I get to meet the most passionate, purpose-driven classroom and campus leaders in the nation, who are doing the most heroic work on the planet. It's incredibly rewarding.

Recently a small school district in rural Oklahoma requested that I come work with their teachers. After we settled on the date, I sent over the contract along with my presentation requirements. The superintendent immediately called back to let us know,

> We have everything you need, but we don't have a stage. We're a really small school in a really small town. We don't even have an auditorium. We're just going to put all the teachers in the lunchroom and there's no stage in there.

I explained to him,

> Sir, I don't need a stage because I'm a Prima Dona. I need a stage because I'm only 5'3" tall! If people are going to be able to see me, I need some help – like 12 to 18 inches of vertical help.

He laughed and said, "I'll put my woodshop teacher on it. He's been teaching here for over 50 years and he solves most of our problems. He'll figure it out."

Early in the morning on the day of the event, I walked into the small lunchroom and I saw a group of teenage students standing in a circle. As I got closer, I realized they were circled up around a stage. Without a doubt, it was the most beautiful, custom-built stage I had ever seen. The kids were beaming with pride as one explained the details of their work:

> The top is a 4x8 sheet of plywood we took off the back of some shelves we built for a teacher last semester. We tacked carpet on top of it to protect the plywood because we're going to put it back on the shelves when you're done. That sheet of plywood is sitting on top of a bunch of step stools we built for the library so the little kids could reach books. Then, we got some construction paper and stapled it around the edges to make it look nice for you.

It truly was an amazing stage built by an even more amazing group of proud young adults.

As the students left the lunchroom, they all stopped and shook hands with an older gentleman who was standing by the door. As I headed back to introduce myself, I said, "Let me guess. You're the woodshop teacher whose been solving most of the problems around here for over 50 years and those are your students."

"Guilty as charged." He replied. I said, "Those are obviously incredible kids who take a great amount of pride in their work." He answered back, "Well, they should because I teach them to take pride in everything they do."

Before he left, I thanked him for his service. "I appreciate all you do for kids and teachers around here. Building bookshelves, and step stools, and stages, I know all that means a lot to everyone in your school family."

Just before he stepped out the door, he turned back to me and said, "Sir, no need to thank me. Those kids do all the work, not me. I don't build shelves, or step stools, or stages. I build great people."

Wow. For over a half century this man has dedicated his life to using his classroom for one, singular purpose: Building great people of character. And, as I watched him walk out to his pick-up truck, I thought about those millions of inspiring, heroic educators who also show up every day to do whatever it takes to have a positive, lifelong impact on our leaders of tomorrow who are sitting in our classrooms today. I'm overwhelmed with appreciation for those incredible educators. And, that includes you.

87

Tiny, Incremental Changes Lead to Monumental Impact

I once read that, on average, our students have about 60,000 thoughts per day. If you're like me, when you just read that, you thought to yourself, "Not my kids! At the most, maybe 17 total thoughts per day." But, if you add up the number of hours a kid is awake each day; then, multiply that by 60 minutes per hour; then, multiply that by 60 seconds per minute, it will make more sense to you.

When I came across that research, I immediately realized just how big of a task I had sitting before me in my classroom. The research put a metric in place for what I was trying to accomplish each day. I thought to myself, "I have such limited time to work with these kids and I'm trying to completely change 60,000 thoughts? That doesn't seem feasible!" It felt overwhelming. It honestly felt impossible.

But then I read the rest of the study. It said that of those 60,000 thoughts per day, the analysis shows that 90% of those thoughts are basically the same handful of thoughts over and over and over. And, once I figured out the math, I got crazy inspired.

Think about the power that lies in shifting just one, single thought or belief that a kid holds to be true. Imagine the impact you can have. Think about the kid who doubts himself who now, because of you, believes, "I have the potential and capacity to successfully learn whatever I want to learn." Think about the kid who doesn't feel loved who now, because of you, believes, "I deserve to be loved." Think about the kid who doesn't feel like she matters who now, because of you, believes, "I'm a significant, influential force for good in this world. I matter."

Those new, empowering thoughts will reoccur thousands of times in the mind of kids, not just throughout the day, but, more importantly, for the rest of their lives.

It's those tiny, incremental shifts in the minds of your kids which, over time, pile up to make a monumental difference in the lives of your kids.

88

Begin with the End in Mind

My last teaching assignment was at a high school. I had the most coveted teaching position on campus. I taught leadership classes, oversaw mentoring programs, and sponsored student council along with a variety of other student organizations. It was a high school teacher's dream come true.

Because of my unique position on campus, I attended a lot of student conferences. In fact, I was traveling with busloads of kids to about a dozen conferences every school year. Each time we showed up for a conference, we had a tradition we would follow. The kids called it "pre-gaming."

Just before stepping inside the conference venue, I would find something to use as a makeshift stage. Sometimes it was bench. Sometimes it a cement wall. More than once I remember climbing onto the shoulders of the biggest, tallest kid in the class. As soon as I knew all the kids could see me, I would launch into our tradition.

As loud as I possibly could, I would yell out to my kids, "Of all the conferences you have ever been to, at which did you learn the most?" In unison, they would yell back, "THIS ONE!" With as much volume as I could possibly muster, "Which conference had the best speakers?" Again, they would yell back, "THIS ONE!" I continued, "At which conference did you give the most?"

"THIS ONE!"

"Which did you connect with other students the most?"

"THIS ONE!"

"Which did you love this most?"

"THIS ONE!" Finally, I would yell one more time, "Tell me why!" Simultaneously, and in unison, they would all yell back, "BECAUSE I GAVE THE MOST AND ENGAGED THE MOST!"

The reason I started this tradition with my kids is obvious. First, I wanted them to experience the concept of beginning with the end in mind. I would tell them,

> If you wait until after the conference is over to decide what you thought about it, it's too late to do anything about it. You can't change the past. Let's decide what we think about the conference before it ever even begins, that way we can affect it. You may not be able to change the past, but you absolutely can impact the future.

Second, I wanted my kids to understand that it's their responsibility to get the most out of a learning experience. I wanted them to learn that the more you give to an experience, the more you'll grow from the experience.

At the end of the day, before loading back onto the buses to head home, I would get back on my "stage" and, at the top of my lungs, I would yell, "Which was the best conference you have ever been to?" With whatever remaining energy they had left over from a long day they would yell back, "THIS ONE!" I would follow up with, "Tell me why!" They would yell back, "BECAUSE I MADE IT THE BEST!"

On one of our rides home, a student asked, "How come we only 'pre-game' for conferences and not other stuff?" Wow. What an amazing question. So, from that point on we started 'pre-gaming' for everything we did – class, afterschool meetings, community service events, all of it. Maybe I wasn't sitting on the shoulders of the biggest kid in class and screaming at the top of my lungs. (Although, that did happen on more than a few occasions.) But, we always made a point to take just a couple of minutes to decide how we were going to take responsibility for making this moment, on this day, the very best it could possibly be.

89

There's No Tired Like Teacher Tired, But It's Totally Worth It

It was a Friday night after a grueling week in the classroom and my wife insisted that we go out for dinner with some neighbors and their kids. As I'm sitting at the table in the restaurant surrounded by friends, family, margaritas, and enchiladas, my vision is starting to lose focus, keeping my head upright is becoming really challenging, and the weight of my eyelids is just about unbearable. No, I didn't yet have a sip of margarita, I was just exhausted. The guy sitting across from me laughs as he says, "You look like you're about to pass out. Do you need me to find a pillow so you can just lay down and take a nap on the floor?" In my mind, I thought about answering, "YES! Thank you! That would be amazing! I would love to stretch out on the floor with a pillow!" But instead, I replied, "Sorry, but it's been a long week at school and I'm beyond tired. I'm 'teacher tired'." That's when he actually said what most non-teachers think, but never say:

> You know, I honestly don't understand why teachers are always posting on social media about being so tired. We all work hard at our jobs. We are all tired. I just don't get why teachers think they feel a special kind of tired. It's not like you are all Alaskan crab fisherman working 72 hour shifts on the frozen Bering Sea.

He doesn't get it. But, I honestly can't blame him. There's no way for him to get it. He's never taught, and he never will teach, so there's no way for him to experience what it's like to be "teacher tired." I'll agree, it's definitely not the same kind of tired an Alaskan crab fisherman would feel. Nor is it the same as working a manual labor job eight hours a day in the blistering heat. Is "teacher tired" somewhat about physical exhaustion? Of course, it is. We all found that out when the Fitbit was invented, and we discovered just how many miles we were putting in during a typical school day. But, our brand of tired has more facets than others.

More so than the physical exhaustion, consider the intellectual exhaustion we experience in our classrooms. We're constantly trying to analyze and solve issues created by the most confusing, complex, and mystifying creatures on the planet – CHILDREN! But, it's so much more than that. It's also the intellectual exhaustion created by the responsibility and pressure of making thousands of daily decisions that we know will shift the trajectory of a kid's life. We're all aware that even the tiniest, most simple decision that we make for a student will have lifelong implications. Sure, we may not be able to see the implications of our decisions right now, but every teacher knows that with every decision we make for a kid, eventually, there will be a consequence. That consequence could be incredibly positive, or it could be incredibly negative. Carrying the weight of that enormous, overwhelming responsibility is extraordinarily draining for educators.

What about the emotional exhaustion that we experience? Someone would actually have to ride the constant roller coaster of emotions that we experience on a daily basis to truly understand it. It's the euphoria of seeing a child reach his full potential, immediately followed by hearing the awful medical diagnosis of another child. It's the feeling of love and compassion when our classroom family finally comes together and connects on a deep level, immediately followed by the frustration of being yelled at by an uninformed, irrational, and hateful parent. It's the pure joy and excitement of witnessing the metamorphosis of our students becoming kind and compassionate people, immediately followed by the crushing sadness and anger as the school counselor shares with you why Child Protective Services has removed one of your students from her home and the unspeakable horror this young girl has endured for years.

And, of course, the lack of sleep. If it were just physical, we would all be able to lay down at night a drift off peacefully into eight hours of refreshing, blissful slumber. But, for teachers, we toss and turn as we think about all the things that still need to be handled in our classrooms. We worry about those kids who we know are hungry and alone in their homes. We second guess all that we said and did in our classrooms. We constantly mull over ideas for how we can do a better job for our students. We feel guilty for all that didn't work out as well as we had hoped it would. We worry about the teachers who we know are currently struggling even more than we are. And, that's just scratching the surface of a very, very long list.

No one outside of the classroom will ever understand what it's like to be "teacher tired." It's simply not possible. And, that's fine. I completely understand it and I'm ok with it. But, what I hope they do realize is that even though we're so tired that our heads might actually fall face first into our refried beans as we're trying to enjoy a Friday night meal with friends and family, along with the unending struggles and challenges and heartache, teaching is absolutely, 100%, totally worth it.

90

There's a World of Difference between Classroom Leadership and Classroom Management

I'm not sure when or where the phrase "classroom management" originated, but I have a feeling it was more than a few decades ago. I'm certainly no educational historian, but I would guess that the concept of classroom management was probably developed during a time when there was way less divorce, more families were attending church together, communities felt a collective responsibility to raise children, and there wasn't a constant stream of uncensored graphic ideas and images being constantly fed directly into the heads and hearts of our children through social media. At the time, maybe classroom management was all that was required. Today, I'm not sure classroom management is enough.

Classroom management is all about creating processes and procedures for delivering content in an effective and efficient matter. It is often a "rules-based" atmosphere where the focus is on the teacher assigning tasks and students completing tasks. Usually, it's a highly regulated environment where instruction is controlled and delivered by one person. And, the effectiveness of a well-managed classroom is determined by one thing: Respect for authority.

Obviously, as you read through that description of classroom management, and consider the personality of our current generation of kids, a couple of challenges will become glaringly obvious. First, this is a generation of kids who do not immediately respect authority. It takes a combination of genuine authenticity and a lot of time to create the feeling of mutual respect in today's student. But, maybe the biggest challenge of all with a classroom based solely on the rules-based, traditional management model is that when kids are non-compliant – which, at some point, will happen – it can only lead to some form of punishment. That is, we must use punishment to modify behavior so kids conform to the rules and procedures. However, it doesn't take long for even a brand-new teacher to realize that we can punish just about any kid into temporary compliance. But we can't punish a kid into the feeling of a deep sense of commitment between the student and teacher that will last throughout the school year. Does a well-managed classroom where kids are learning efficiently require processes and procedures? Absolutely, 100% it does. However, for it to be truly effective and lasting, there must be more to it than that. There must be a sense of leadership, as well.

Classroom leadership is more about developing and adopting a set of core classroom principles based on input from every member of the classroom family. Rather than managing a class to create rules for the purpose of assigning and completing tasks, leadership comes from a place of facilitating conversation and working together to design a shared, clear vision and an inspired mission for what the classroom family wants to accomplish together. Leadership is not an authoritative environment of you versus me, but rather a loving, trusting, mutually respectful, and connected environment of we.

Do kids need a teacher who's an expert in classroom management? Of course, they do. However, you and I also know that this is a generation of kids who need so much more than management. They desperately need a leader in their lives. They need a leader who is going to guide their classroom family based on the principles of love, meaningful relationships, compassion, grace, acceptance, and accountability. Because for most of our kids, the style of leadership they experience in their classroom family today, will become their style of leadership for leading their own families tomorrow.

91

Thank You for Your Faithfulness

Having spent over 25 years in the educational field, I understand how isolated and lonely you may feel at times. You may also feel like you are all but invisible. But, know that you are not. Your administration may not say it enough and your students may not tell you enough but they are thankful for all you do. Yet, it really makes your day when an administrator or a student does take the time to let you know. It seems to make all the hard work worthwhile.

I know you never hear it enough, so I wanted to make sure to thank you for your faithfulness to your calling; to your purpose. As I travel the country speaking to teacher groups, I make sure that I emphasize how thankful I am that each and everyone of you enters the classroom each day to impact the lives of our youth. Even though some days you may not feel like you are making an impact.

I am reminded of the words of Mother Teresa, who said she was not called to be successful but to be faithful. She spent most of her life living among and taking care of the poor and indigent in Calcutta, India. She never sought fame or fortune, but to be faithful to her calling. I am sure there were times when she didn't feel successful or that she was making a difference, but she did make a difference. I think this is a healthy perspective to have. In our culture everyone is focused on success, but if we focus on our calling, on our purpose, then we are already successful. Never underestimate the difference you make and know that you are appreciated. Know that your students thank you and appreciate you as well, even if they never find the words to express it!

92

Laughter Is . . .

If you are as old as I am, you remember a very popular book about the first days of school and one of the recommendations in it was not to let your students see you smile until Thanksgiving. While I agree that Thanksgiving break is definitely something to smile about, I didn't like the idea of waiting until then to smile at my students.

I think the flaw in this thinking is that children love to laugh. I have heard experts say that children laugh up to 400 times per day but adults only laugh about 40 times per day. While, I don't know if the numbers are exact, in my experience I don't think they're far off. And if this is an important part of childhood, wouldn't it make sense that it would be a big part of building relationships with those children?

I taught middle school science and at least several times per week I would open class with a funny story or joke. I always found this to relax the students, get their attention, and make learning fun, all at the same time. Laughing is a way to make class more fun and it helps you connect to students on a personal level. They see you as a real person and not just their teacher.

Laughter also has many positive values, such as stimulating the release of dopamine, and stimulating goal-oriented motivation and long-term memory. And we know all the health benefits of laughter such as reducing stress hormone levels, boosting the immune system, and lowering blood pressure.

So what is laughter? Well laughter is medicine and laughter is learning. So, while you may not laugh 400 times today, it certainly won't hurt to try!

93

Being All-In

The term All-in means fully committed to or involved in something. But another meaning is tired or exhausted. When it comes to teachers, I think one is just as accurate as the other. We know teachers seemingly put all their time and energy into their students. Whether it is working late on weekends, or volunteering for just one more thing your administrators asks of you.

I also know as a new teacher, there are times when things will seem overwhelming and you will have to work more than you should. I also know veteran teachers who spend many extra hours at work as well. But, I will let you in a secret, being All-in doesn't mean that you need to work or be available 24/7. You do not have to be a martyr. As I write this, we are in the middle of a pandemic and many of you are working from home right now. And the tendency is to stay near the computer and respond as quickly as possible, regardless of the hour, to keep students and families engaged. But you have to set limits. Whether you are at school or home, you have to set limits. Remember All-in doesn't mean giving your all, all the time, because that is burnout, not All-in. I think one of the reasons that we have 10% teacher attrition every year is because of this issue with burning out. A few tips to help you keep from burning out are; to remember not everything needs to be graded immediately and not everything needs done before you go home; giving students responsibility in the classroom can save you a lot of time; and finally, set aside time for you and your family, if you work late a couple of days per week, make sure you leave on time the other days. Remember you want the best for your students, but also remember All-in doesn't mean exhausting yourself to the point that you leave the field. Your students need you, but they need the best you!

94

Teaching Is a Privilege

The one thing I miss about teaching in the K-12 classroom is the students. In the moment, it is easy to get caught up in the curriculum, technology, standards, and testing and forget to enjoy the time with your students. Yes, I even miss the ones who drove me crazy some days.

What makes me miss those moments is that all our students become our kids. I have seen some of my former students all grown up and many laugh about how they were in middle school. It is almost like watching your child grow up, especially when they tell you how much they enjoyed your class or they remember something you did. If you are a veteran teacher you are probably thinking of some of those students right now. The ones who taught us as much as we taught them. The ones who made us laugh and even made us cry. If you are a new teacher, you may not have experienced this yet, but you will.

The importance of seizing the day or enjoying the time with students is that I saw it as a privilege to serve them. Teaching is in many ways a privilege. Parents entrust you with their child for a whole year or maybe two. Children trust you to take care of them, inspire them, encourage, them and yes even love them! Some may be harder to reach than others, but they are all worth the effort. Every student has talents and a purpose. It is a privilege to spend part of their life with them helping them become the best version of themselves that they can. Never take that for granted. Because one day you will miss those laughs, those moments, and those students. Seize the day!

95

Don't Ask Your Kids to Do a Better Job; Demand Them to Be Incredible

I spent my entire teaching career in Texas. If you don't already know, or if you haven't read or watched Friday Night Lights, Texas high school football is a pretty big deal. It's actually more than a big deal. If you've never attended a Texas high school football rivalry game between two small towns, it would be impossible to comprehend the role that football plays in Texas communities. Let me put it to you this way: I was driving through Port Neches, TX on the way to speak at the high school and I saw gift shop with a sign in the window that read, "Faith, Family, & Football." At the bottom of the sign, just for clarification, it read, "But not in that order on Friday nights!" That's how big of a deal high school football is in Texas.

From the moment I became a teacher I have been fascinated with high school football coaches. I've seen so many coaches, both in the classroom and on the field, who are world class, master teachers. They're experts at their craft and I studied them. I watched intently as these men served, not just only as coaches and teachers, but also as the dad their players didn't have at home. I watched as these men worked tirelessly – sometimes 60, 70, 80-hour weeks – to put their players in the best possible position to compete. I observed these men teach and coach, not just in the classroom and on the field, but in every moment of every day, no matter where they were. I observed how these men built rock-solid relationships with their players so that they could set incredibly high expectations for them. And, in watching all this, I decided early on that I wanted to serve my students the same way I saw coaches serving their players.

One day after school, I decided to go watch football practice. As I sat in the bleachers, I was amazed at how these coaches were able to inspire their players to practice with such intensity and focus in the 103-degree blistering Texas heat. As I drove home that evening, it dawned on me that not once did I hear a single coach ask for less than a player's absolute best. As I thought more about it, I could hear their voices echoing in my mind: "Here we go, men. You are champions. Let's practice like it ... I demand an incredible effort from you ... The time to be phenomenal is right now ... I know you're capable of greatness, keep pushing yourself ..." Constantly, throughout the entire practice, coaches were instilling these messages into the hearts and minds of their players.

As I thought more about it, what those coaches were demanding of their players on the football field was very different than what I was asking of my students in the classroom:

> Can I please have your attention? ... Let's have a good class today ... Make sure you do a good job on that ... Can you do a little bit better than that for me? ... That's fine, it's good enough.

I spent years requesting kids to do a "better job." But, maybe because of the low-quality relationships that I built with my students, only asking kids to do "better" was the best I was able to do. Those amazing coaches that I studied were able to build deep, strong relationships with their players, which gave them the right to demand the very "best" their kids had to offer. Earning the right to demand kids to do their "best" produces vastly different results than only asking kids to do a "good job."

Deep down inside, every great teacher wants the same thing. We all want to have a dramatically positive, lifelong impact on the lives of our kids. I'm not sure that kind of impact will ever be the result of a classroom where students are simply asked to do a good job by a teacher they barely know. However, I'm absolutely certain that kind of impact will definitely happen when our students' best efforts are demanded by the person they positively know loves them.

96

Don't Ever Let Someone Make You Feel Crazy for Wanting What's Right for Kids

Maybe it's because I have developed somewhat of a following that people think I must love social media. But, to be honest, I'm really not a fan. However, I am thankful for it. Because it was with the advent of Facebook and Twitter that I discovered I wasn't completely insane.

I'll explain.

Have you ever had the experience of being in an after-school faculty meeting; your principal at the front of the room presenting on whatever the current topic happens to be; and, everyone, including you, is smiling and nodding in agreement. Then, suddenly, your principal says something that sounds completely insane. Startled by her statement, you think, "Wait, what? That's crazy." But, before you raise your hand for clarification, you look around the room only to discover everyone else is still smiling and nodding in agreement with what you thought was completely insane. So, you choose to stay quiet while you wonder, "Am I the only one who thinks that idea is crazy?"

Here's just one example of the many times I've personally had that experience. I can remember sitting in the middle school library late in the afternoon at a faculty meeting. The topic was student tardiness. Our school had a tardy problem unlike anything I had ever seen. It was especially baffling to me because I didn't have a tardy problem in my class. With the exception of once or twice a week, my students were on time every day. In the faculty meeting, everyone – for the most part – was engaged when the principal declares, "We are going to attack this tardy problem with a policy called 'Tardy Time-Out'. Starting tomorrow, if a kid is late to class, they will be denied entry to the classroom and immediately sent to the cafeteria where they will remain for the rest of the class period." Immediately, I think, "Wait, what? So, now we're going to take a chronic tardy problem and turn it into a chronic absence problem?" But, before I could raise my hand, it became obvious that everyone is clearly happy, enthusiastically nodding in agreement, and some teachers even applauded. As our principal continued, what I thought was a bad idea got even worse. She said, "Then, the following school day, rather than going to that class, those students who were tardy must meet back in the cafeteria. Then, they will be sent back to your classroom halfway through the class period." Now, with even more people applauding, I thought to myself,

> Wait. So, instead of a kid being a few minutes late to class, now they're going to be absent for one and a half class periods? Then, the day after they're tardy, the kid won't remember to go to Tardy Time-Out, so they're going to be tardy to Tardy Time-Out. Eventually, my lesson is going to be interrupted when they send the kid back halfway through the class period. And, I'm going to have to work extra hard to try to catch the kid up on all they missed?

Again, I look around and everyone clearly loves this idea which I happen to think is completely insane.

It only takes a few of these experiences for you to start wondering. "Is it me? Maybe I'm the one who's crazy!" And, that's why I'm thankful for social media.

Social media has provided a place for teachers around the globe to build community with other like-minded educators – especially those of us who, for years, have thought to ourselves, "Am I the crazy one?" Once you find, follow, and share with these teachers who are just like you, you discover that we're NOT the ones who are crazy. We're the ones who truly understand our students are just kids. As obvious as that statement may sound, it seems to me that lots of educators tend to forget that fact. Whether your students are 7 years old, or in the 7th grade, or 17 years old, they're just kids. Do all kids need a set of boundaries that include rules, procedures, and accountability? Absolutely, they do. But, when it comes to developing and nurturing successful young scholars of strong character, it also requires a lot of compassion, grace, understanding, and empathy.

Take the time to surround yourself – whether in-person or online – with those kinds of educators who truly understand children. It will provide you with the confidence and courage to know that you're not completely insane. You just want what's right and best for kids. And, your students deserve to finally have someone raise their hand, stand-up, and speak-up for what's right and best for them.

Please, let that someone be you.

97

Please, Just Give the Kid a Pencil

I was welcoming and greeting my first period freshman students at the door of my classroom when I saw Krystal hurrying down the hall. The tardy bell rang when she was still about four classrooms away. As she looked up and made eye contact with me, I could tell she was wondering if she had to go get a pass from the office for being late to first period. I called down the hall, assuring her, "It's ok. Don't worry about it. Come on, I've got you."

When she met me at the door, I could tell she was exhausted. Her clothes were wrinkled, her hair was unbrushed, she didn't have her backpack, and the dark circles under her eyes were more prominent than usual. I knew exactly what it all meant.

"Was it your turn last night?" I asked. "Yes, sir." she answered as she came through the door and slumped into the closest chair. I went and retrieved one of my boxes that contained a variety of school supplies – pencils, pens, markers, sticky notes, paper, etc. – and put it next to her desk. "Hey, just do the best you can today." I told her. "If we need to catch you up on anything, you can just swing by at lunch tomorrow. Cool?"

"Ok, cool." she replied.

Krystal might be one of the most amazing people I've ever met. At 14, she's the oldest of six girls in a single parent family. Her mom waitresses the early breakfast shift and late dinner shift and cleans houses in between. When I asked Krystal if it was "her turn," that's code, referring to the nights when it's her responsibility for taking care of the house; feeding her five sisters; making sure their homework is done; getting the girls bathed; making sure everyone has clean clothes for the next day; and getting them tucked into bed. Like I said, she's a phenomenal kid.

Later that day, I was walking to the front office when I noticed Krystal standing in the hallway. Just then, her teacher swung the door open, stepped into the hallway, pointed her finger in Krystal's face, and yelled, "I am tired of you coming to class unprepared! All I ask is that you bring a pencil and you can't even do that. You're completely irresponsible, and I am no longer going to put up with it!" Her teacher slammed the door behind her as she left Krystal standing in the hallway.

"Completely irresponsible," the teacher called her. Unbelievable.

Nothing could be further from the truth. I had never seen a more graphic example of a teacher who spent absolutely no time building a relationship with a student. She obviously knew literally nothing about Krystal's life outside of the classroom. If she did, she would know that the list of responsibilities that Krystal handles is longer than that of most adults.

As teachers, of course we want to use our classrooms as a place to instill successful habits and traits in our students. We all want to inspire a sense of responsibility in our kids. But, if we are to do that, we must know our kids. We must know the details of what is happening in their lives, both inside and outside the classroom. We must understand our kids, not just academically; but also, personally, and emotionally, as well. Yes, the classroom should be a place where kids develop habits of success – like responsibility. However, there are hundreds of other ways to teach responsibility that doesn't include school supplies – something which not all kids have equal access to. Remember, all kids do not share the same childhood. Please, just give the kid a pencil.

Since you're a teacher, I'm sure you're wondering, "What did you say to Krystal after her teacher went back in the classroom?"

Well, first I opened the door and whispered to her teacher, "I'm going to take Krystal with me for this period." And then I immediately closed the door so she didn't have a chance to say anything back. Then, Krystal and I went to the front office, we ate chips from the vending machine, and we chatted about life and what an amazing job she was doing as a big sister. We also set-up a system where she would take with her whatever supplies she needed for the day when she left our first period class each morning.

Also, since I took the time to build a solid relationship with Krystal's school counselor, I was also able to get her a new teacher for that class period. One that was better suited for where Krystal was in life and what she needed right then.

98

Your Kids May Forget the Content, but They Will Remember the Experience Forever

I was so excited when I saw the two names at the top left corner of the envelope – Adam and Jessica. And, when I opened the envelope and pulled out the invitation to their wedding, I was so happy I couldn't help but smile. I even laughed as I remembered having them both in my class 15 years earlier when they were 8th graders. Even back then, I can remember thinking, "These two kids are definitely going to get married." All the other kids in class thought so, too. I can remember Adam and Jessica coming through the door and kids would start singing the melody to the wedding march.

The wedding was beautiful and perfect, and the reception was basically a reunion for our 8th grade class. As we sat around reminiscing, each kid (now an adult, but will forever be my "kids") took a turn recalling a story from our year together. "Do you remember the time that …" Or, "What about the time when …" Or, "Remember when we all …"

I sat there in awe as they could recall the most minute of details about what happened in class even after 15 years. They remembered details as if it all happened just yesterday. They recounted exactly what happened, when it happened, who was there, what was said, what happened next. They could remember everything.

While all this was happening, I pretty much sat there quietly and participated by smiling, and nodding, and laughing, and agreeing with what everybody remembered. Because, I honestly couldn't remember the vast majority of what they talked about.

In our classroom, 15 years earlier, what seemed like insignificant events to me, became lifetime memories for my kids.

It was just one more reminder that our kids might not remember much about the content we teach them, but they will forever remember the experiences we provide for them.

99

Every Word, Look, and Gesture
Can Impact a Child Forever

I was recently in a vintage toy store and saw a game I remembered from my childhood. The game is called The Last Straw or, some people refer to it, simply as The Camel Game. The game is based on the idiom, "the straw that broke the camel's back." For those of you who were not alive in the late 60s and early 70s, the game consisted of a brown, plastic camel that came in two separate pieces and was held together at the center by a rubber band. The camel stood upon yellow wheels attached to its feet. At the separation in the center, between its two humps, hung a yellow basket on both sides of the camel. The object of the game was not to be the one who broke the camel's back.

To play the game, players would take turns placing "pieces of straw" (which were small, colorful sticks varying in weight and thickness) into the camel's basket. As the basket became heavier and heavier with each additional piece of straw, the camel would begin to sag in the middle at the separation. If you were a strategic player, you would place your heaviest pieces of straw into basket first, saving your lightest pieces of straw for the end when the camel was most fragile. Eventually, as one too many pieces of straw was added to the basket, the plastic camel would no longer be able to handle the weight as its back would fully separate and the camel would come crashing down. That last piece of straw was, quite literally, "the one that broke the camel's back."

When I think about that childhood game, it reminds me of working with kids. Kids are carrying around all the negativity, hurt, and emotional trauma they have ever experienced in their personal baskets. But as teachers, there's no way for us to truly know or understand the details of what's in a kid's basket – how full it is, how traumatic it is, how painful it is, how heavy it is. Thank goodness that some of our kids have extremely light baskets with not much of anything to carry around. However, for lots of our kids, their baskets are extremely full and traumatic and painful and heavy. Those kids with the most in their baskets are the most fragile. They are on the brink of breaking. And, as a result, just like in the game, it can be the tiniest piece of "straw" placed in a student's personal basket that can break a kid.

For all educators, the most scary and stressful part of teaching is how simple and easy it is to innocently and unintentionally break a kid who is carrying around the heaviest basket. It could be something as simple as the kid seeing a look of annoyance on the face of their teacher. Or, a just inadvertent eyeroll of frustration. Maybe a loud voice of anger.

The most simple, smallest, accidental, unintentional act really can break a kid.

It's impossible for us to know which kids are carrying the heaviest of baskets. So, with all that we're pouring into our kids throughout the school day, let's make sure it's thoughtfully and gently done with empathy. And, just maybe, we can replace some of the hurt, the heartache, and pain with experiences love, compassion, and kindness.

100

"You Don't Just Make a Difference, You Leave a Legacy"

Never underestimate the importance of your role as a teacher or the legacy that you leave behind. Consider my cousin Tammy, who was a teacher for over 25 years. She taught special education and regular education classes at various times throughout her career. Regardless of the class or grade level, one thing was always true, she loved her students, and they loved her. Whether it was a hug or school supplies, she always had what the students needed. She always made sure they were having a good day, even if it was just in her class.

Sadly, Tammy passed away a couple of years ago from cancer, but that was not the end of her story. Her last request, when she was faced with her own mortality was for friends and family to bring backpacks full of supplies to her funeral instead of flowers. She was always thinking of others first and said there were many students in need within the community.

At the funeral, there were over 100 backpacks lined along the chapel pews and upfront. About 50 teachers were honorary pallbearers and after the service, they formed a long line for the casket to be carried through to the hearse. I actually posted a picture of the backpacks sitting by the pews in an empty chapel on twitter and it went viral, reaching millions of people worldwide! Every major media outlet in the world ran a story on what they called the teacher's last request, backpacks in lieu of flowers. It was one of those feel good stories that resonated with everyone; not just teachers.

A teacher who lived in relative anonymity for her whole life became a source of inspiration for the world with her final lesson, which was to put others first. Countless students she had taught through the years spoke of the positive impact she had on them and how she changed their lives. People from all around the world sent backpacks to her school district because they felt such a connection to her teacher heart. I even had teachers from around the world message me and say that they were going to ask for this as their final request as well.

So, on those tough days, remember, you aren't just making a difference, but you are planting seeds that will sprout in the lives of your students. You are creating a legacy that will live on through them long after your journey is completed.